HUMAN DEVELOPMENT BOOKS:
A SERIES IN APPLIED BEHAVIORAL SCIENCE

Joseph and Laurie Braga, *general editors*
*University of Miami Medical School*

HUMAN DEVELOPMENT BOOKS is a series designed to bridge the gap between theory and research in the behavioral sciences and practical application by readers. Each book in the series deals with an issue important to the growth and development of human beings, as individuals and in interaction with one another. At a time when the pressures and complexities of the world are making increased demands on people's ability to cope, there is a need for tools that can help individuals take a more active role in solving their own problems and in living life more fully. Such information is not easily found or read by those without previous experience or familiarity with the vocabulary of a particular behavioral field. The books in this series were designed and executed to meet that purpose.

ELISABETH KÜBLER-ROSS is a psychiatrist, a world-renowned leader and authority on death, and the author of *On Death and Dying, Questions and Answers on Death and Dying,* and *Coping with Death and Dying,* the latter a series of five cassette tapes available from Ross Medical Associates, Flossmoor, Ill.

BOOKS IN THE SERIES

*Growing with Children,* by Joseph and Laurie Braga
*Growing Older,* by Margaret Hellie Huyck
*Learning and Growing: A Guide to Child Development,*
    by Laurie and Joseph Braga
*Culture and Human Development: Insights into Growing Human,*
    by Ashley Montagu
*Death: The Final Stage of Growth,* by Elisabeth Kübler-Ross
*Children and Adults: Activities for Growing Together*
    by Joseph and Laurie Braga

# DEATH
## The Final Stage of Growth

ELISABETH KÜBLER-ROSS

A SPECTRUM BOOK

PRENTICE-HALL, INC., Englewood Cliffs, New Jersey

*Library of Congress Cataloging in Publication Data*

Main entry under title:

Death : the final stage of growth.

(A Spectrum book)
Includes bibliographical references.
1. Death—Psychology—Addresses, essays, lectures.   I.   Kübler-Ross, Elisabeth.
BF789.D4D44      155.9'37      75-9688
ISBN 0-13-197012-7
ISBN 0-13-196998-6 pbk.

A SPECTRUM BOOK

11 12 13 14 15

Printed in the United States of America

Prentice-Hall International, Inc., *London*
Prentice-Hall of Australia Pty., Ltd., *Sydney*
Prentice-Hall of Canada, Ltd., *Toronto*
Prentice-Hall of India Private Limited, *New Delhi*
Prentice-Hall of Japan, Inc., *Tokyo*

# Prayer for Healers

LORD,
    Make me an instrument of your health:
where there is sickness,
    let me bring cure;
where there is injury,
    aid;
where there is suffering,
    ease;
where there is sadness,
    comfort;
where there is despair,
    hope;
where there is death,
    acceptance and peace.


GRANT that I may not:
so much seek to be justified,
    as to console;
to be obeyed,
    as to understand;
to be honored,
    as to love. . . . .
for it is in giving ourselves
    that we heal,
it is in listening
    that we comfort,
and in dying
    that we are born to eternal life.

*Prayer of St. Francis*

(modified by Charles C. Wise)

Dedicated to—

Manny, Kenneth, and Barbara, whose love makes this work possible, and in memory of my mother, who died on the very day this manuscript was finished, September 12, 1974.

Thanks to Doug McKell for his untiring assistance in putting this manuscript together, to Rosalie Monteleoni, who keeps my spirits up and my office functioning, and the Rubins, whose support continues to flow when I need it most.

Joe and Laurie Braga have not only been the initiators of this book but have spent innumerable hours to "shape" it and have done so with the love that only true friends can put into a task like this.

# Contents

Foreword                                                                x

Preface:
A Journey into the Realm of Death and Growth   xiv

**1**
Introduction                                                            1

**2**
Why Is It So Hard to Die?                                               5

THE ORGANIZATIONAL CONTEXT OF DYING
*Hans O. Mauksch*

DEATH IN THE FIRST PERSON
*Anonymous*

**3**
Death Through Some Other Windows                                      27

DYING AMONG ALASKAN INDIANS: A MATTER OF CHOICE
*Murray L. Trelease*

THE JEWISH VIEW OF DEATH: GUIDELINES FOR DYING
  *Zachary I. Heller*

THE JEWISH VIEW OF DEATH:
GUIDELINES FOR MOURNING
  *Audrey Gordon*

THE DEATH THAT ENDS DEATH IN HINDUISM
AND BUDDHISM
  *J. Bruce Long*


4

Dying Is Easy, But Living Is Hard                    73

  LIVING UNTIL DEATH: A PROGRAM OF SERVICE
  AND RESEARCH FOR THE TERMINALLY ILL
    *Raymond G. Carey*

  FUNERALS: A TIME FOR GRIEF AND GROWTH
    *Roy Nichols and Jane Nichols*

  A MOTHER MOURNS AND GROWS
    *Edith Mize*

  ONE WOMAN'S DEATH—A VICTORY AND A TRIUMPH
    *Dorothy Pitkin*


5

Death and Growth: Unlikely Partners?                 117

  DEATH AS PART OF MY OWN PERSONAL LIFE
    *Elisabeth Kübler-Ross*

  LETTER TO ELISABETH: DEDICATED
  TO CAROL
    *Bal Mount*

LOUIE
*Shirley Holzer Jeffrey*

FOR MY WIFE WANDA: LOVE WILL NEVER GO AWAY
*Orville Kelly*

# 6
# Death· The Final Stage of Growth 145

DYING AS THE LAST STAGE OF GROWTH
*Mwalimu Imara*

Ω
# Omega 164

Resources 169

Index 177

# Foreword

Death is a subject that is evaded, ignored, and denied by our youth-worshipping, progress-oriented society. It is almost as if we have taken on death as just another disease to be conquered. But the fact is that death is inevitable. We will all die; it is only a matter of time. Death is as much a part of human existence, of human growth and development, as being born. It is one of the few things in life we can count on, that we can be assured will occur. Death is not an enemy to be conquered or a prison to be escaped. It is an integral part of our lives that gives meaning to human existence. It sets a limit on our time in this life, urging us on to do something productive with that time as long as it is ours to use.

This, then, is the meaning of *DEATH: the Final Stage of Growth*: All that you are and all that you've done and been is culminated in your death. When you're dying, if you're fortunate enough to have some prior warning (other than that we all have all the time if we come to terms with our finiteness), you get your final chance to grow, to become more truly who you really are, to become more fully human. But you don't need to nor should you wait until death is at your doorstep before you start to really live. If you can begin to see death as an invisible, but friendly, companion on your life's journey—gently reminding you not to wait till tomorrow to do what you mean to do—then you can learn to *live* your life rather than simply passing through it.

Whether you die at a young age or when you are older is less important than whether you have fully lived the years you have had. One person may live more in eighteen years than another does in eighty. By living, we do not mean frantically accumulating a range and quantity of experience valued in fantasy by others. Rather, we mean living each day as if it is the only one you have. We mean finding a sense of peace and strength to deal with life's disappointments and pain while always striving to discover vehicles to make more accessible, increase, and sustain the joys and delights of life. One such vehicle is learning to focus on some of the things you have learned to tune out—to notice and take joy in the budding of new leaves in the spring, to wonder at the beauty of the sun rising each morning and setting each night, to take comfort in the smile or touch of another person, to watch with amazement the growth of a child, and to share in children's wonderfully "uncomplexed," enthusiastic, and trusting approach to living. To live.

To rejoice at the opportunity of experiencing each new day is to prepare for one's ultimate acceptance of death. For it is those who have not really lived—who have left issues unsettled, dreams unfulfilled, hopes shattered, and who have let the real things in life (loving and being loved by others, contributing in a positive way to other people's happiness and welfare, finding out what things are *really you*) pass them by—who are most reluctant to die. It is never too late to start living and growing. This is the message delivered each year in Dickens's "Christmas Carol"—even old Scrooge, who has spent years pursuing a life without love or meaning, is able through his willing it, to change the road he's on. Growing is the human way of living, and death is the final stage in the development of human beings. For life to be valued every day, not simply near to the time of anticipated death, one's own inevitable death must be faced and accepted. We must allow death to provide a context for our lives, for in it lies the meaning of life and the key to our growth.

Think about your own death. How much time and energy have you put into examining your feelings, beliefs, hopes, and fears about the end of your life? What if you were told you had a limited time to live? Would it change the way you're presently conducting your life? Are there things you would feel an urgency to do before you died? Are you afraid of dying? Of death? Can you identify the sources of your fears? Consider the death of someone you love. What would you talk about to a loved one who was dying? How would you spend your time together? Are you prepared to cope with all the legal details of the death of a relative? Have you talked with your family about death and dying? Are there things, emotional and practical, that you would feel a need to work out with your parents, children, siblings before your own death or theirs? Whatever the things are that would make your life more personally meaningful before you die—do them now, because you *are* going to die; and you may not have the time or energy when you get your final notice.

In this book, Dr. Elisabeth Kübler-Ross has gathered a spectrum of views on the subject of death and dying that will guide you in your search for the meaning of life and death. Whether you are a dying patient; a relative, friend, or loved one of someone who is dying; a member of one of the helping professions involved with terminal patients; or simply a person who desires to learn to live more fully through better understanding death's meaning, this book will provide insights that should help you find peace in life and death.

From her sharing of her own life experiences that have provided her with the direction and strength necessary to open our eyes and hearts to the realities of death and dying; to discussions of the issue from the points of view of ministers and rabbis, doctors, nurses, funeral directors, and sociologists; to presentation of other cultures' views of death and dying; to the sharing of feelings of persons dying or experiencing the death of someone they love, the author has assembled and integrated a collection of perspectives on death and dying that should stimulate both your thoughts and feelings about the subject. Whoever you are and whatever your stage of growth, you'll find something here to light your way on life's journey.

None of us knows what awaits us after this life. But you will hear the thoughts, beliefs, and hopes of other cultures and of individuals within our culture. You will be able to observe the growth of one woman as she shares her experiences of the death of her only son. You will learn how some have found ways to work through their grief over a loved one's death and see the ways that you can help yourself and others in this process. You will learn what factors make a difference in how a person faces death, and gain insight into the type of personality characteristics that predict acceptance of that fate. And you will see how all these things can be applied in your day-to-day life now, even if you have another fifty years on this earth.

But it is not enough simply to intellectualize about the subject of death and dying. You must go beyond the words and become involved in the feelings those words evoke for you. As you read, it is important that you become aware of and examine your own emotional reactions to the accounts that are presented. Then stop to think about those feelings as they relate to your dealing with (1) the death of others—friends, family, or dying patients you serve as a member of the helping profession, (2) your own death, and (3) the way you are living your life.

Because of the courage and love for humanity that Elisabeth Ross has shown in bringing to wide public awareness the much avoided subject of death and dying, we are all being given an unparalleled opportunity—to discover life's true meaning through coming to terms with death's place in the spectrum of human development, and thus to learn to use our gift of life as happily and productively as possible. If you face a problem, whether you are able to solve it or not, you will grow. Death is a problem in our society. We urge you to accept the challenge and opportunity available to you now of dealing with this problem, of facing it squarely. You will grow through the experience.

JOSEPH L. BRAGA
LAURIE D. BRAGA
*General Editors*

# Preface: A Journey into the Realm of Death and Growth

At the time when this book is published, ten years will have passed since my first interview of a young dying patient in Colorado, in front of a group of medical students.

This was by no means planned or preconceived, and no one at that time had the slightest idea that this kind of "Death and Dying Seminar" would become known nationwide and be copied throughout the country and abroad. Being a foreigner, I never dreamed of writing a book on this topic; I simply tried to do a good job as a new instructor in psychiatry. Coming from Europe, I was impressed by the lack of understanding and real appreciation of psychiatry among medical students. I must admit that many of the teachers were just plain boring and simply repeated the contents of psychiatric textbooks to the young medical students who would have been better off reading the original texts themselves. Others flooded the students with terminology which made no sense to them, and so they either switched off the teacher's voice or dozed through the lectures.

To teach psychiatry under a distinguished and admired professor* was a challenge to me, and I searched for ways to keep my students awake and interested during the two-hour lecture assignment. Determined not to speak about psychiatric disease entities, the thought occurred to me that death and dying would be an interesting topic with which all students eventually had to come to grips. I desperately searched for literature, but there was little to be found. I finally put my first lecture together, a compilation of rituals and customs in other cultures, a way to cope with death from the American Indians to modern Western man. In order to bring this to a clinical and more relevant level I followed the lecture with an interview of a 16-year-old girl suffering from acute leukemia and I asked some medical students to sit and question her with me. The patient did most of the talking;

---

* Dr. Sydney Margolin, Denver

the students were frightened, nervous, stiff, or very academic—display-ing more anxiety than the dying girl.

Much to my relief none of the students fell asleep. They sat quietly and remained absorbed in their own thoughts and feelings about the mystery of death—which they were to face as future physicians (though this did not dawn on them until the moment of that young girl's sharing).

Much later, in Chicago, where these seminars became a weekly occurrence, another medical student so wisely described what she had never noticed in all the years of her training: "In all my experiences as a medical student in the dramatic and desperate resuscitations, I can hardly recall seeing a dead person. Part of it is the result, no doubt, of my own desire to have as little to do as possible with corpses. However, part of it is also due to the remarkable disappearing act that occurs as the body is cleverly whisked out of sight. In all the hours, day and night, that I have spent in this hospital, I have never caught a glimpse of any point of the procession, from the exit of the cart from the patient's room to its destination, be it morgue or hearse."

For many years I continued to ask terminal patients to be our teachers. They volunteered for this and were quite aware that many students would watch and hear them. For the sake of more privacy we sat behind a two-way mirror, seen and heard by physicians, nurses, clergy, social workers and others concerned with the dying patient. Some observers could hardly tolerate the anxiety these interviews stimulated in them; others sat in awe and admiration of the courage and openness of these patients. I don't think any of the hundreds of students who sat and listened were untouched. Old memories surfaced, accompanied by a new awareness of their own fears as something to be understood and not judged. We all grew in many ways, most importantly perhaps in an appreciation of life itself.

One of my most sensitive students recalled some of these memories: "I remembered G., one of my best friends. I was twenty when G. was hospitalized for a check-up. He meant a lot to me, especially during my teenage years. I guess, like all teenagers, I felt that my parents did not understand me, but somehow G. always did. . . . I met him in church as an altar boy. As I grew older he seemed to be the only person I could really talk to."

This student later described how he was studying music, how a critical illness left him alive but without a voice to sing, and how it was G. who encouraged him never to give up. He regained his voice again, only to be faced with another tragedy: "G. was hospitalized the next fall for a biopsy. It was cancer. The doctor told him that he may have six months to live. I called on him at home regularly in the months that followed, and gradually the truth started to sink in. He became thinner and weaker and finally was confined to bed, a skeleton with white hair. I could not take it anymore and left. I never again saw him alive. He died several weeks later. Even in death he remembered me. He knew that as a junior member of the choir I would never get to sing Presentor's aria, and he requested in his funeral instructions that I sing it at his funeral. His funeral was a festival. People he had helped at one time or another came from all over the hemisphere. I could not believe that one man could become so involved with so many people. And I guess I have never forgiven myself for deserting him during those last weeks."

The student who wrote these memories a few years ago is now one of the most helpful ministers I know for those who are critically ill or bereaved. It is through such losses and with the help of caring and teaching people that we can face death rather than avoid it.

A young social worker described for us her reasons for wanting to attend the Death and Dying seminars. She had worked for years with the elderly and never became comfortable in this work until she attended the seminars and listened to what our patients had to say: "One of the main reasons why many of us avoid any talk of death is the awful and unbearable feeling that there is nothing we can say or do to comfort the patient. I had a similar problem in working with many aged and infirm clients in the past years. I always felt that old age and sickness was so devastating, that although I wanted to communicate hope to them, I only communicated despair. It seemed to me that the problem of illness and death was so insolvable and therefore these people could not be helped. . . . I think that this seminar has helped me to see that life did not have to end in mental and physical agony. Just listening to Mr. N. (one of our interviewed patients) describe the death of his father-in-law as an almost beautiful event, and then seeing Mr. N. himself coping so well with his own approaching death gave me a feeling that it really is possible to resolve the crisis of dying in a dignified way. In working with any patient, there must be a goal toward which you both are striving and some belief that movement to resolution or comfort is possible. It seems to me from observations of the interviews that listening itself is a comfort to these patients. I think another great help a social worker can give is to the family of the dying patient—not so much in the way stressed by so much of the casework literature (homemaker, financial aid, etc.)

but in helping them to relate better to the patient. Mr. N. wanted to talk about his illness to his wife and she to him. But they were each afraid to cause the other pain and did not know how much the other knew. With reassurance from the staff, Mrs. N. was able to broach the subject with her husband, and they were then able to share and to be a source of comfort to each other—instead of each suffering alone. This seminar has certainly helped me to realize this—that people need not suffer alone when they are dying. It is possible to help them share their feelings and in this way find some relief and peace."

Many of our patients passed from a stage of shock and disbelief to the ever-recurring question "Why me?" Many of our dying young people tried to find a meaning in their suffering. Victor Frankl has written: "Let us now consider what we can do if a patient asks what is the meaning of his life. I doubt whether a doctor can answer this question in general terms. For the meaning of life differs from man to man, from day to day, and from hour to hour. What matters therefore, is not the meaning of life in general, but rather the specific meaning of a person's life at a given moment."

Later on he clarifies something that perhaps each one of us should realize more often: "As each situation in life represents a challenge to man and presents a problem for him to solve, the question of the meaning of life may actually be reversed. Ultimately, man should not ask what the meaning of his life is, but rather must recognize that it is he who is asked. In a word, each man is questioned by life; and he can only answer to life by answering for his own life; to life he can only respond by being responsible."

Having seen hundreds of terminal patients grow through the crisis of their illness, becoming responsible for their own life, one wonders if Frankl himself would ever have reached this high level of wisdom and understanding, compassion and richness if he had not had the experience of facing death a thousand times in the death camps of World War II!

A young minister, who was looking forward to his clinical counseling duties with mixed-emotions, summed up his feelings after the Death and Dying seminar, a course he had signed up for as a preparatory step:

I consider this opportunity a totally new experience for me and one that I anticipate with a mixture of excitement, curiosity and dread. I will take five "rules" with me into this experience, "rules" that I know will change as I experience my self in relation to them:

*Number 1:* Concentrate on the dying patient not as a case history, but as a part of a one-to-one relationship. This attitude requires disciplines which are new to me. First, I must try to be myself. If the dying patient repulses me, for whatever reason, I must face up to that repulsion. I also must let the other person be himself, without projecting my own feelings of repulsion or hostility. Since he really is a human being, I suspect that he needs the same type of love and care that I do.

*Number 2:* Honor the sanctity of the human being. Just as I have "secret" values, fears, joys, so does he. His God, Christ, and Value-system have been hard-won over a life-time of curiosity, struggle, and hope, as have mine. My faith is that when we talk to each other about ourselves, we will find something in common. And the commonality is that "wondrous ingredient" that allows people to share their lives. That sharing is the realization of our humanness.

*Number 3:* Honoring the sanctity of the individual forces the counselor to let the patient "tell him" how he feels. The minister must, in this situation, "let the patient be." This simple rule does not imply granting all of the patient's demands and jumping whenever the patient wants the counselor to jump. If the counselor is honest, he will face his bias and accept it as his personality rather than apologize for it and try to hide it. The belief that "I know what's best for the patient" is not true. The patient knows best.

*Number 4:* I must continually ask myself "What kind of a promise am I making to this patient and to myself? If I can "realize" that I am trying to save this person's life or to make him happy in an unendurable situation, then I believe that I am typically human and hopefully can stop trying to attempt both. If I can learn to understand my own feelings of frustration, rage, and disappointment, then I believe I have the capacity to handle these feelings in a constructive manner. It is in this realization that human wisdom lies.

*Number 5:* My fifth and last rule, the rule that covers all four others, is expressed in the Alcoholics Anonymous Prayer:

> God grant me the serenity to accept the things I cannot change,
> the courage to change the things I can,
> And the wisdom to know the difference.

What all of us hoped for during the first few difficult and lonely years of our Death and Dying seminar is perhaps best summarized in this prayer. Students came from numerous disciplines: Medicine, Nursing, Social Work, Sociology, Philosophy, Theology, and Psychology. Each one of them came for a different reason, I am sure. Some felt truly uncomfortable in their work with dying patients and tried to find ways of understanding their frustrations and anxieties. Others knew that no exams or tests were given and came out of curiosity. Still others came "not knowing why" but obviously with some unresolved grief or death experiences in their own life. The students were never a problem. They filled the classroom long before the classes started and often continued to discuss the interviews long after I left.

The patients who were asked to serve were no problem either. They were often quite grateful to be "useful," to feel that someone needed them rather than the other way around. When we started to talk they quickly overcame their initial shyness and rather quickly shared with us the fantastic loneliness they felt. Strangers whom we had never met shared their grief, their isolation, their inability to talk about their illness and death with their next-of-kin. They expressed their anger at the physician who did not "level" with them, at the minister who tried to console them with the too often repeated phrase "It is God's will", or at friends and relatives who visited them with the inevitable "Cheer up, it's not so bad." We learned to identify quickly with them and became much more sensitive to their needs and fears than ever before. They taught us a great deal about living and dying, and they appreciated our asking them to be our teachers.

Our main problem was with the physicians. They first ignored the seminar; later they would refuse to give us permission to interview their patients. They often became quite apprehensive or hostile when we approached them. Many colleagues said to me quite indignantly: "You cannot interview this patient. She is not dying. She may even be able to go home once more." It was obvious that they missed the whole point of the seminar. We certainly did not wish to talk to dying patients during the last day of their lives. How could we ever bring families together in the very last moment? How could we help to alleviate the loneliness and fear of our patients when we were not allowed to see them before they were on their actual death bed? How could we teach our students what a patient goes through if we only saw them in their last few days? We could not convey to our colleagues that we are all dying—that we all have to face our finiteness long before we are terminally ill. This is perhaps the greatest lesson we learned from our patients: *LIVE, so you do not have to look back and say: "God, how I have wasted my life."*

Mrs. M. was 71 years old. One of her recurring statements was "If I could only do my life over, and know what I know now, I would do it so differently!" When she enlarged upon this, it came through that her whole life appeared to her as having been mostly wasted. Her life had been filled with anxiety because of several failures in marriage, several job changes, and many moves. Now in the hospital, looking back at her life, she saw herself without roots, friends, or meaningful relationships, and her fears were magnified by the awareness of her limited life expectancy. In the midst of this emptiness and sorrow came the invitation to our seminar. Someone needed her. We asked her to teach us what she would change, if she were given a second chance. We became involved with her, and she started to trust us and confide in us. We became friends. We began to look forward to our visits with her, and we left enriched and aware that we should live today and not postpone it, lest we die alone. How fortunate that she had a physician who trusted us and who allowed us to visit her before her very last days!

The real change occurred when our seminar became "famous." For several years I held my Death and Dying seminar almost inconspicuously, not marked in any program, yet always filled with students. It was after it became an accredited course and was publicized by the university's PR Department that magazines like TIME and LIFE became curious and visited my classroom. Little did I know that the LIFE article was to change thousands of lives, including my own.

It was on a cold and rainy fall day when I interviewed Susan, a lovely girl of twenty-one, who was in our hospital with acute leukemia. She talked openly about her wish not to have a funeral and to donate her body to a medical school. She talked about her fiancé, who appeared to have deserted her when the diagnosis was confirmed (though she still denied that fact), and she also mentioned her awareness that her days were counted.

Deeply impressed by her frankness and lack of fear, I invited her to attend my seminar so that my students could hear and learn from her. Upon entering my classroom she opened the conversation with the statement: "I know my chances are one in a million; today I only wish to talk about this one chance." Needless to say, we changed the topic of that day's seminar to "On Life and Living." We simply asked her what it would be like if she could live. She shared her hopes with us that she could still graduate in June and get married in July: her bargaining was that she would wait for five years to have children in order to be sure that she would live to raise them. Occasionally I realized while listening to her that the LIFE magazine people were behind the screen window, watching their one and only Death and Dying seminar. But I had no time to worry about them. I was too involved with Susan, who seemed to have the strength to face her limited lifespan and at the same time was able to "live in a temporary denial" in order to dream of all the things that would have made her life meaningful. Needless to say, we simply shared her dreams.

After the tremendous publicity we received in LIFE, my own life was never again the same. My first reaction was concern for Susan. I had no idea how she would feel seeing page after page of her pictures in an internationally known magazine, a true testimonial to her courage and her inner beauty. The first copies of LIFE were delivered to me during the night. I had to reach her before the magazine was in the hospital newsstand! I left for the hospital in the earliest morning hours, anxious about her response. She took one look at her picture and blurted out "Gosh, that's not a very good picture of me!" How healthy and normal she was in all this turmoil. She was little impressed by her sudden notoriety. She was simply looking forward to going home "once more" as she stated, "to enjoy every moment to its fullest." She did leave the hospital once more. She did get her beloved puppy-dog, and she did live every minute to its fullest. I think Susan lived more in the last few months of her life than the 71-year-old woman did in seven decades. But Susan did something else that she was barely aware of: Through her sharing with us, through the LIFE article, she touched thousands of lives all over the world. Letters flooded my house from every corner of the world—letters of faith, love, caring, hope, and encouragement. A letter from a man on death row, a scribbled paper from a very old man who had not written a letter in years, hundreds of letters from dying children, teenagers, and grownups—who took courage from her courage and loved her without ever seeing her in person.

After Susan's death on January 1, 1970 the world seemed to change. I am not sure if it was her impersonal death alone in the intensive care unit or the parents' lonely agony in the waiting room that night that stirred us all. I became determined to talk about death and dying until we were able to change some of the attitudes in this death-denying society.

After her death I was no longer insulted or even impressed by the physicians' negative and sometimes hostile attitudes. I began to see their side as well as ours. I began to realize that our medical schools prepare them almost exclusively in the *science* of medicine and give them little help in its *art*. I made a strenuous effort to reach the medical students, who were ready and willing to learn more about their role in the care of the patient who is beyond medical help. After each interview we took the patient back to his room but continued to discuss among ourselves what we had learned. Suddenly clergy and physicians shared their own anxieties; nurses felt comfortable for the first time to express their frustrations over their limited freedom to tell the patient what they knew. Social workers and occupational therapists discussed their fears and tribulations, and we finally succeeded in an interdisciplinary dialogue which was so necessary for the sake of the staff and the patients.

Mail continued to come in; invitations came from all over the country to speak in hospitals, seminaries, nursing schools and other institutions. Colleges and high schools followed, and before long the market seemed to be flooded with books and articles on the needs of dying patients. Films and videotapes were made, and almost every theological seminary in the country included some aspects of ministry to the dying patient in their curriculum.

It has been ten years now since my first lecture on Death and Dying. During this last year I have traveled 200,000 miles all over the United States, Canada, and Europe. Invitations have come from as far away as Korea—my own personal needs and the needs of my children and family prevent me from accepting this last. I have received more letters than I can count from dying patients, newly bereaved persons, and members of the helping professions—letters with the most personal expressions of love and fear, hope and despair, appreciation and awareness of facing their own death.

I will stop the traveling at the end of this year. I have done what I was destined to do—I have been able to function as a catalyst, trying to bring to our awareness that we can only truly live and enjoy and appreciate life if we realize at all times that we are finite. Needless to say I have learned these lessons from my dying patients—who in their suffering and dying realized that we have only NOW—"so have it fully and find what turns you on, because no one can do this for you!"

I do not know what the future holds for me, but one thing I know: working with dying patients is not morbid and depressing but can be one of the most gratifying experiences possible, and I feel now that I have lived life more fully in the last few years than some people do in a whole lifetime.

Elisabeth Kübler-Ross

# 1
# Introduction

Death always has been and always will be with us. It is an integral part of human existence. And because it is, it has always been a subject of deep concern to all of us. Since the dawn of humankind, the human mind has pondered death, searching for the answer to its mysteries. For the key to the question of death unlocks the door of life.

In times past, human beings died in numbers too large for most of us to comprehend, the luckless victims of war and pestilence. Just living was an accomplishment of fate, and death was a feared and dreaded enemy who struck indiscriminately at rich and poor, good and bad alike. The thinkers of the past, pious people and representatives of Enlightenment wrote books about death. They tried to rob it of its strangeness and terror by studying it seriously. They tried to find its meaning in the lives of human beings. And at the same time that they clarified the meaning of death, they also contributed to understanding the significance of life.

Now, when humankind is surrounded by death and destruction as never before, it becomes essential that we study the problems of death and try to understand its true meaning.

For those who seek to understand it, death is a highly creative force. The highest spiritual values of life can originate from the thought and study of death.

We can see from studies of different religions that the thought of death forms the kernel of all creeds, myths, and mysteries. The selections on "The Jewish view of death" and the one entitled "The death that ends death in Hinduism and Buddhism" show you how different views of death mold the lives of those who hold those views. The most persistent questions that human beings explore through their myths and religions are those pertaining to rebirth, resurrection, and a life hereafter: Is there another life after this one? And if there is, what is the relationship between that one and the way you live this one? It's not just a question of good and evil, heaven or hell, as you will see when you read the selection on Hinduism and Buddhism. It's also a question of growth and the level of enlightenment reached in this lifetime.

From the Indian Vedas (sacred texts of the earliest phase of Indian religion, 3000 years ago) to the words of our contemporary thinkers, the aim of all philosophers has been to elucidate the meaning of death, thus helping human beings to overcome their fear. Socrates, Plato, and Montaigne have taught: to philosophize means nothing more than to study the problem of death. And Schopenhauer called death "the truly inspiring genius of philosophy."

Thomas Mann once said: "Without death there would scarcely have been poets on earth." Any person who studies poetry through the centuries can verify this. The first epic, the Babylonian Gilgamesh, and the first-known lyric poem of world literature, a poem by Sappho, dealt mainly with death. From then until now, no great poet has existed who failed to dedicate some of his most beautiful verses to death. And all of them touched the deepest secret of life while talking about death.

"No thought exists in me which death has not carved with his chisel," said Michelangelo. From the Egyptian, Etruscan, and Attic beginnings of art to modern surrealism, death has played an important part.

And as in philosophy, literature, and art, death was also the great inspirer of music. The first songs were funeral dirges, and the great music of Bach, Gluck, Mozart, Beethoven, Schubert, Liszt, Verdi, Mahler, Moussorgsky, and the modern composers frequently has death as its leading motif.

Death is, however, not only the inspirer of artistic imagination. It has strongly influenced the ethical attitude of human beings as well. Death was the great instructor of those noble characters in history whom we venerate as heroes, saints, or martyrs of science.

I hope to convey one important message to my readers: namely, that death does not have to be a catastrophic, destructive thing; indeed, it can be viewed as one of the most constructive, positive, and creative elements of culture and life.

This book attempts to familiarize the reader with some other aspects of death and dying, with the viewpoints of other people, other cultures, other religions, and philosophies. I hope that one thing comes through all these pages—namely, that all people are basically alike; they all share the same fears and the same grief when death occurs. We are finite little beings who could help each other if we would dare to show that we care, if we maintain some compassion and, last but not least, if we stop being judgmental and try to learn WHY people behave as they do in crisis. For this we need a sound understanding not only of human (general) behavior, but also of the individual's cultural and religious background.

In the decades to come we may see one universe, one humankind, one religion that unites us all in a peaceful world. It is up to each of you to lay the groundwork for this future generation, by making an attempt NOW to comprehend and care for your fellow humans, no matter what their creed, color, or philosophy. Through understanding that in the end we all share the same destiny—that just as surely as we are alive, so we will die—we may come also to understand that in life also we must be as one, aware and appreciative of our differences and yet accepting that in our humanness, we are all alike.

# 2
# Why Is It So Hard to Die?

Dying is an integral part of life, as natural and predictable as being born. But whereas birth is cause for celebration, death has become a dreaded and unspeakable issue to be avoided by every means possible in our modern society. Perhaps it is that death reminds us of our human vulnerability in spite of all our technological advances. We may be able to delay it, but we cannot escape it. We, no less than other, nonrational animals, are destined to die at the end of our lives. And death strikes indiscriminately—it cares not at all for the status or position of the ones it chooses; everyone must die, whether rich or poor, famous or unknown. Even good deeds will not excuse their doers from the sentence of death; the good die as often as the bad. It is perhaps this inevitable and unpredictable quality that makes death so frightening to many people. Especially those who put a high value on being in control of their own existence are offended by the thought that they, too, are subject to the forces of death.

But other societies have learned to cope better with the reality of death than we seem to have done. It is unlikely that any group has ever welcomed death's intrusion on life, but there are others who have successfully integrated the expectation of death into their understanding of life. Why is it so hard for us to do this? The answer may lie in the question. It is difficult to accept death in this society *because* it is unfamiliar. In spite of the fact that it happens all the time, we never see it. When a person dies in a hospital, he is quickly whisked away; a magical disappearing act does away with the evidence before it could upset anyone. But, as you will read later in various contexts, being part of the dying process, the death, and the burial, including seeing and perhaps interacting with the body, is an important part of coming to grips with death—that of the person who has died and your own.

We routinely shelter children from death and dying, thinking we are protecting them from harm. But it is clear that we do them a disservice by depriving them of the experience. By making death and

5

dying a taboo subject and keeping children away from people who are dying or who have died, we create fear that need not be there. When a person dies, we "help" their loved ones by doing things for them, being cheerful, and fixing up the body so it looks "natural." Again, our "help" is not helpful; it is destructive. When someone dies, it is important that those close to him participate in the process; it will help them in their grief, and it will help them face their own death more easily.

It *is* hard to die, and it will always be so, even when we have learned to accept death as an integral part of life, because dying means giving up life on this earth. But if we can learn to view death from a different perspective, to reintroduce it into our lives so that it comes not as a dreaded stranger but as an expected companion to our life, then we can also learn to live our lives with meaning—with full appreciation of our finiteness, of the limits on our time here. I hope that this book will help you understand death and dying better and will make it a little less hard for you to die and a little easier for you to live.

Most people in our society die in a hospital. This, in itself, is one of the primary reasons that dying is so hard. The first selection of this chapter explores, from a sociological point of view, the hospital as a depersonalizing institution which is not, by definition, set up to meet the human needs of people whose physiological condition is beyond the hospital's capability for successful intervention; these patients represent a failure of the institution in its life-sustaining role, and there is nothing in the system that provides for human nurturance to the soul when the body is beyond repair. The other selection is a moving poem by a young student-nurse who is dying. Having spent time in the hospital as a practitioner and now as a patient, she issues a plea to those who minister to the sick and dying to step away from their professional roles and reach out as human beings to those who need them.

# The Organizational Context of Dying

## Hans O. Mauksch, Ph.D.

*In our modern technological society, dying is something you do in a hospital. But hospitals are efficient, impersonalized institutions where it is very difficult to live with dignity—where there is no time and place in the routine to deal with the human needs of sick human beings. In the following selection, Dr. Mauksch explains why it is that hospitals, by definition, are rarely responsive to the special needs of people who are dying. Hospitals are institutions committed to the healing process, and dying patients are a threat to that defined role. The professionals in hospitals have specified expectations and routines to carry out; these simply don't work with dying patients. This is a threat to the professionals' roles and creates feelings of inadequacy which are inconsistent with their defined roles as people who can deal effectively with disease. There is no room in the prescribed roles of professionals for them to behave as human beings in response to their dying patients. The history and reasons for the kinds of constraints that exist in the hospital organization are explored by Dr. Mauksch, and he proposes that this need not be so. I think you will find this perspective on the hospital setting (for all people, whether they are dying or not) a very valuable one.*

The predominant number of deaths these days occur within the hospital, the institution created by society to support the healing services. Actually, to be historically correct, there was a period in the early phases of the development of this institution when the hospital, indeed, was the institution for people who were either poor and indigent or who were dying. As the science and technology of medicine and of the other health professions have experienced the dramatic growth and development which characterizes the health field in the twentieth century, the whole flavor, aura, culture, and

"The Organizational Context of Dying," by Hans O. Mauksch, Ph.D. © 1975 by Hans O. Mauksch. This essay was written especially for this volume. Used by permission of the author.

social organization of the hospital has shifted from an institution devoted to charity and to those who die to an institution which is fundamentally committed to healing, to curing, to restoring, and to the recovery process.

In a differentiated society like our modern, highly complex one, we tend to endow the occupants of social roles and institutions with mandates which denote their purpose, their function, and their values. The current roles of the health professions have emerged through their own achievements and through the growth of social expectations. In the midst of the current technological emphasis on the success story of healing, the patient whose disease cannot be cured, the human being who is dying is inexorably perceived to be a failure to the health professions—a failure of the mandate given to the professionals and to the institutions. The organizational context of dying within the hospital must be understood as an institutional response to an event which today is identified as a failure, although it also remains a reminder of the limits of medical knowledge and capabilities.

A second, more subtle dimension of the organizational context of dying is the different focus required by the needs of the dying patient compared to the needs of the patient whose illness is about to be cured. As a social scientist within the medical setting, I seek to remind physicians and other health professionals that the human being who happens to be ill is indeed an integral part of the disease process and that his or her interactions are crucial to the cure, the care, and the future life of the patient. In the case of the dying patient, the current culture of the hospital, which emphasizes the disease process and the diseased organ, is counterproductive to the needs of the dying patient. Dying is a total experience, and at the point of dying, the diseased organ ceases to be the primary issue.

There is a third dimension to the climate of dying. In his book *Passing On: The Social Organization of Dying*, David Sudnow suggests that physicians and nurses, in their behavior and in their attitudes, demonstrate a sense of discomfort and a sense of guilt when facing human beings who, entrusted to their care, terminate their lives in the face of all efforts.[1] Those of us who are committed to recovery, to healing, to cure cannot avoid, within the context of the hospital culture, sensing that we have failed when one of our patients dies.

---

[1] David Sudnow, *Passing On: The Social Organization of Dying* (Englewood Cliffs, N.J.: Prentice-Hall, Inc., 1967).

There are several ways in which this sense of guilt, this sense of failure can be understood. It suggests the search for whether everything had been done, whether there were other kinds of resources that could have been invoked, whether all diagnostic and therapeutic means had been employed.

There is a second way in which one can look at this particular issue. There is a mixture of reality and myth in the belief in the continuous growth and expansion of medical knowledge. I have interviewed a number of physicians who, in the face of the death of a patient, raised the question, "Is there someone else, somewhere, who has new knowledge that could have made the difference?" The sense in which every physician feels responsible for the total state of current medical knowledge apparently varies from physician to physician and hospital setting to hospital setting, but it is an important potential cause for the discomfort of the physician and for possible blocks in the relationship between physician and patient.

There is the third haunting possibility that I, the physician, or I, the nurse, may have made a mistake, may have committed an error which contributed to the patient's death. Somewhere within the hospital culture lurks the awesome expectation that, while all other human beings are permitted to make mistakes and to commit errors, physicians and nurses must not. Indeed, the facts suggest that these clouds of possible errors have only limited basis in fact. A number of studies have shown that relatively few errors occur, although when they do they tend to be dramatic. When errors occur they tend to make the rounds of hospital gossip and, sometimes, even make the national press. In a study conducted by me, I found that among 240 so-called "Incident Reports" in an 800-bed hospital over a three months' period, only two of these so-called incidents involved situations in which the patients were physically affected and actually endangered by the error committed.

In order to appreciate the way in which the dying patient fits within the total system of the hospital, we have to recognize that the hospital represents an institution which, in a sometimes misunderstood and sometimes misused way, has to routinize the emergencies of its clients and their varied individual needs. At the same time the hospital is a place which houses a network of different occupations which, although ideally complementary, tend to have inadequate communications and are isolated when they should communicate. In the midst of all this, the dying patient represents a series of human events where the needs of the client cease to be translatable into routines and rituals. It is in this fundamental sense that the dying patient threatens the hospital and its personnel. The routine orders, the predictable activities, when applied to the dying patient, cease to be meaningful, cease to be effective, and, above all, cease to be satisfying either to the people doing them or to the patients who receive them.

It is interesting to note that the hospital and its culture considers death in some way one of its own taboos. In the hospital patients do not die, they expire. Patients do not die in the operating room; rather, the patient is "lost on the table." The language of the hospital suggests that denial, the first of the stages described by Dr. Elisabeth Kübler-Ross,* is also the first and frequently the continuously defended stance of the institution and its personnel. The hospital and its personnel tend to reward the patient for maintaining the denial phase because it protects the hospital personnel from becoming involved and from facing their own feelings. It also protects them from having to communicate with each other, with the patient, or with the patient's family.

This type of appreciation was expressed by a head nurse whom I interviewed shortly after a patient had committed suicide on her ward. This head nurse said with much feeling, "You know, Mrs. X was such a cooperative patient. We all liked her very much." She thought for a

---

* The five stages referred to here are the "stages of dying" formulated and described in detail by Dr. Ross in her book, *On Death and Dying.* They can be briefly summarized as follows:

1. **Denial**—"No, not me." This is a typical reaction when a patient learns that he or she is terminally ill. Denial, says Doctor Ross, is important and necessary. It helps cushion the impact of the patient's awareness that death is inevitable.

2. **Rage and anger**—"Why me?" The patient resents the fact that others will remain healthy and alive while he or she must die. God is a special target for anger, since He is regarded as imposing, arbitrarily, the death sentence. To those who are shocked at her claim that such anger is not only permissible but inevitable, Doctor Ross replies succinctly, "God can take it."

3. **Bargaining**—"Yes me, but . . ." Patients accept the fact of death but strike bargains for more time. Mostly they bargain with God—"even among people who never talked with God before."
They promise to be good or to do something in exchange for another week or month or year of life. Notes Doctor Ross: "What they promise is totally irrelevant, because they don't keep their promises anyway."

4. **Depression**—"Yes, me." First, the person mourns past losses, things not done, wrongs committed. But then he or she enters a state of "preparatory grief," getting ready for the arrival of death. The patient grows quiet, doesn't want visitors. "When a dying patient doesn't want to see you any more," says Doctor Ross, "this is a sign he has finished his unfinished business with you, and it is a blessing. He can now let go peacefully."

5. **Acceptance**—"My time is very close now and it's all right." Doctor Ross describes this final stage as "not a happy stage, but neither is it unhappy. It's devoid of feelings but it's not resignation, it's really a victory."

These stages provide a very useful guide to understanding the different phases that dying patients may go through. They are not absolute; not everyone goes through every stage, in this exact sequence, at some predictable pace. But this paradigm can, if used in a flexible, insight-producing way, be a valuable tool in understanding why a patient may be behaving as he does.

moment, she was quiet, and there were tears in her eyes; and then this nurse turned to me again and said, "Do you know how cooperative she really was? She even committed suicide exactly at three o'clock, so that neither shift would have to be responsible for the consequences."

It is important to recognize that when Dr. Ross speaks of the needs of the patient working through the stage of anger that the hospital as an institution is not designed to absorb and to cope with the patient's anger. Patients are made to feel dependent on their physicians and nurses, are made to feel that they should be grateful for the care that they are given by these "marvelous people." Indeed, this is a feeling shared widely by patients and one that physicians and nurses have become accustomed to expect. Therefore, the patient who tries to express anger does not only communicate a personal need, does not only cry for help, but indeed violates the culture, the rules, the expectations of the institution and thereby threatens the system. Only when physicians and nurses have been taught to view the behavior of their patients as significant symptoms of unique human needs and when they feel it is an integral part of their professional capability and responsibility to respond to these needs, only then will physicians and nurses be able to cope with patients' anger without feeling personally offended and institutionally attacked.

The same comments can be made about the bargaining patient. The hospital professionals are the ones who determine what is good for the patient and they are the ones who know how much this patient can achieve, how much this patient can do, and even know at what rate the patient's disease ought to progress.

The grieving patient—the fourth stage outlined by Dr. Ross— causes guilt and other discomforts. We live in a society in which control of emotions and the display of proper behavior are highly rewarded. We also live in a society in which joining a profession is associated with something called "professional behavior." In either case, the showing of emotions, the sharing of feelings, and, particularly, the showing of such personal indicators as tears are taboos in our society, particularly for professionals and especially for males. The grieving patient, the patient who cries, not only makes us feel guilty, but he also makes us feel scared about our own ability to sustain a relationship without losing the mask identified with a professional stance. In interviews with physicians and with nurses, the fear of crying, the fear of showing compassion, is tragically a block to the display of some of the genuine concern which is present among many who, in their own frustration, have felt conflict between their concern and the mask that they felt they must wear.

The setting of the hospital and the relationship between health professions has been discussed in many publications and has been subject to comment, criticism, and analysis from many quarters. There is one important issue that directly relates to the dying patient. The technical appropriateness which underlies the logic of the division of labor within the hospital ceases to be meaningful in meeting the needs of the dying patient. I should like to suggest the notion of the "transprofessional" domain. Certain skills and certain roles are professional in nature. They involve responsibility, the assumption of deliberate relationships, and the utilization of identifiable skills. However, the transprofessional domain is one which is not owned by any one profession and which is open to and appropriate for any of the available functionaries. The relationship with the dying patient, the privilege of helping the human being who is dying to work through to the stage of acceptance and to help his or her family is something that ought to be the capability of any of the professionals involved in the care of the person in need. Conversely, not everyone dealing with sick and dying people needs to have developed this skill fully. Thus, I am suggesting a type of teamwork, a type of utilization of appropriate human resources which is different from the typical hospital setting. Actually, at times, the attending physician may not be the best person to help the patient to find comfort and peace. After all, many patients feel that in dying they let their own physician down and many physicians, as mentioned earlier, feel uncomfortable about the death of their own patients. The utilization of human resources by calling in those who may be acceptable and appropriate to the patient invokes atypical behavior patterns within the hospital.

A word needs to be said about the clergy. In the hospital, the clergy have only recently regained some meaning, some entry, and some role. The clergy deserve a significant place not only in helping the dying patient but in serving as a resource to the patient's family and, hopefully, to the physician or to other health professionals who are troubled by the burden placed on their shoulders.

It may seem like a facetious point, but it is worth contemplating that the mandate of the clergy contains a safety valve which can help them to perform the functions of assisting the dying person. Clergy are, in all faiths, the spokesmen or the representatives of a higher power. As they may seek to help and to offer support, it is within the context of personal imperfection and lack of complete authority. By contrast, medicine has been given by our society the aura of having the final authority in dealing with health, illness, and life.

My remarks should not be taken as a criticism of the physician but as a comment on the society which has cast onto the shoulders of the physician something which he or she cannot handle without facing difficult moments. The sharp conflict between mandate and reality has been aggravated by the scientific developments which have lured the physician into the laboratory of biochemistry or physiology and which have given him an aura of laboratory-type control over biological processes. In that process, the peculiar imperfection and lack of finality that goes with the human process have been lost from his own culture and certainly from his own curriculum.

Sudnow distinguishes between two ways of looking at death. There are those deaths which are expected and which are part of the anticipated events of a given hospital unit, and then there are those deaths which could not have been predicted, which occurred in settings within the hospital where death is an exception and a rarity. They "simply should not have occurred." The following quotation from Sudnow's book shows how, on a busy ward with severely ill patients, the staff has developed a way of dealing with death.

A: Hi Sue, bet you're ready to go home.

B: You ain't just kiddin'—it's been a busy one.

A: What's new?

B: Nothin' much. Oh yes, Mrs. Wilkins, poor soul, died this morning, just after I got here.

A: I didn't think she'd make it that long. Do we have a full house?

B: Just about. Number two's empty, and seven I think.

A: Mrs. Jones die?

B: I think so, let me see. (Looks at charts.) Guess so. (Turns to other nurse.) Did Mrs. Jones die today?

C: She was dead before I got in to work this morning, must have died during the night.

A: Poor dear. I hardly knew her but she looked like a nice old lady.

A: You look tired.

B: I am. Lucky you, it's all yours.

A: I hope it's a quiet night. I'm not too enthusiastic.

B: They all died during the day today, lucky us, so you'll probably have it nice and easy.

A: So I saw. Looks like three, four, and five are empty.

B: Can you believe it, we had five deaths in the last twelve hours.

A: How lovely.

B: Well, see you tomorrow night. Have fun.[2]

This quotation can be interpreted in many ways. It does show the staff's need to routinize and organize its activities. It shows the degree to which the differential experiences of a number of people who have died have become part of a routine report. The quotation does not entirely reveal the degree to which these nurses either served as helping agents or protected themselves so that they would not get too involved with these patients.

A death on an obstetric ward, where deaths do not normally occur, is a very different experience. I recall the death of a patient who up to the moment of crisis was expected to have a normal child and a normal delivery. A sudden complication resulted in a very rapid death. The physicians, the nurses, and all other personnel were terribly upset. The unspoken fear of the possible mistake or the possible error was all too obvious within the ward. Two of the nurses broke into tears, which caused the physician to become even more upset and angry, since, after all, people in a hospital are not supposed to cry. The unanticipated death not only upset everyone and created an aura of guilt and failure, but it tended to serve as a conflict-creating event among the people involved in the care of this patient. Communications diminished and it was obvious that following the death of that patient nobody trusted anyone else. The ability to communicate was lost when this crisis occurred.

All this leads to one important issue. Dr. Ross, in her description of the patient's needs and the patient's movement through various stages offers a direct challenge to the health professions and to the educational processes by which we introduce our novices into these professions. I have genuine faith that the technological resources, the organizational complexities, and the power of our scientific capability to cure are not incompatible with the skills and the behaviors which are required to help the dying patient. On the contrary, I believe that the technology of care and cure should enable us to free professionals for giving more deliberate and careful attention to using themselves as instruments of help and of support.

These thoughts require changes in the current climate and structure of medical and nursing curricula. They require changes in the culture of our training institutions. It is an old caveat that the

---

[2] Sudnow, *Passing On*, pp. 36-7.

content of the curriculum will not be as influential as the climate within which the curriculum is taught. When we educate people to take care of other human beings, our educational process must convey that we respect those whom we teach so that they may respect their own clients. We must shift from procedure-oriented patient care to patient-oriented procedures. We must shift from the development of merely technically competent practitioners to professionals who see themselves as having the capability to deal with their own feelings and to use them in a deliberate and humanly sophisticated way.

The important thing about the special topic of care of the dying is that it cannot be a skill that is turned on and turned off only when we confront a person during these terminal stages. The skills, the relationships, the attitudes, and the behaviors which are implicit in these needs must be fundamental to the total network of relationships with all patients. This applies to clients whether they are seriously ill or whether they are recovering and are about to return to healthy functions in society. The entire network of relationships with patients is subject to much more deliberate concerns, improvements, and possible impact than is frequently allowed in the medical curriculum or in the day-to-day practices of patient care.

In a study conducted to determine the patient's view of the patient role, we sought to explore the patient's perception of this relationship and of their own place in the hospital.[3] It involved in-depth interviews with approximately ninety patients and usually several interviews with the same patient.

I am reminded of the very beginning of our research when we sought permission from attending physicians to interview patients who were severely ill, particularly patients shortly after a myocardial infarction. We were met with indignation and with the question, "How dare you bother such sick patients?" We finally found a physician who gave us permission to try.

These interviews were undertaken with some degree of trepidation. It took some time before we discovered that the fear of catastrophe was rarely cause for real concern. I should hasten to add that the kind of interviews we conducted were, of course, cautious, open-ended, and were conducted to permit the patient to talk about what they were ready to talk about. In many instances, severely ill patients welcomed us and thanked us because it seemed to diminish their own tensions to

---

[3] Daisy M. Tagliacozzo and Hans O. Mauksch, "The Patient's View of the Patient Role," in *Patients, Physicians, and Illness*, edited by E. Gartly Jaco (New York: Free Press, 1972).

have the chance to talk and to have someone there who intently listened and showed interest and concern.

We chose to limit our study to patients with gastrointestinal and cardiovascular diseases. Among other things, we wanted to find out whether these two conditions made a difference in the way patients perceived their roles.

In interviewing patients and in analyzing our data, we concluded that in some way the patient in the hospital is made more dependent on the institution than either the inmate in prison, the student in school, or the new employee in an industry. Erving Goffman, the well-known sociologist, speaks of the "stripping process" [4] by which he describes the incorporation of persons into those institutions which embrace the individual totally and which provide procedures and rituals which strip the person of his autonomy, identity, and his distinguishable separate status. This applies to the military service, it applies to the convent, it applies to the mental hospital, but it also applies to the patient in the general hospital, at least to a significant degree.

In the modern hospital, the patient is frequently admitted to a private or semi-private room. The nature of the hospital, its architecture, design, and procedures all tend to discourage the patient from forming a patient community and an interaction system with other patients. Not being able to form informal groupings with peers who help to interpret the institution diminishes the power of the client. Shared informal rules and expectations help clients to share experiences and modes of coping. Through informal communications, patients seek to determine which behaviors are likely to be rewarded and which are likely to be sanctioned by the functionaries of the institutions.

For purposes of dramatizing the process by which the diminishing of the personal autonomy and identity takes place, let us assume that I had been in the office of my private physician two days ago. He confirmed the prescription which I had been taking for some time now. He had his technician do a variety of laboratory tests including urinalysis, examination of a blood sample and various other kinds of diagnostic tests. Yesterday, I was informed that some of the tests' results warranted admittance to the hospital for further work-up. His office had made the reservations for me, and I was asked to report to

---

[4] Erving Goffman, *Asylums: Essays on the Social Situation of Mental Patients and Other Inmates* (Garden City, N.Y.: Doubleday & Co., 1961).

the hospital at three-thirty this afternoon. Let us now go through my experiences.

Much has been written about the fact that when one arrives at the admissions desk of the hospital, waiting is the order of the day. Waiting in itself can be an expression of power by the institution which makes you wait. The filling out of forms, although necessary, can add to the climate of personal surrender. Time, of course, has different meanings in different cultures. In Latin America, the length of waiting time might have a very different meaning than it does in Anglo-Saxon countries. Time has a different meaning in different portions of the United States and different meanings in rural or urban settings. Whatever that may be, the experiences of waiting at some point become a communication. The medical profession, the hospital, and other health professions have been successful in conveying to the public that waiting in the hospital, waiting in the physician's office is almost an expected norm and is the price we pay for the privilege of obtaining health services.

My comments are not meant to imply criticism of the procedures themselves but rather to suggest that procedures, although necessary, have psychological by-products and tend to imply a world of meaning which we must take into account to recognize what happens to human beings who become patients. It is obviously necessary that we identify patients and that we protect patients from errors in medication. However, placing the little plastic band on the arm of the patient as part of the admitting process is an expression of property rights and, in a way, is like branding cattle on behalf of the owner. It means that "we now take possession of you."

A messenger takes us to our room. Once we are admitted to the hospital, we may not walk unescorted even though we may be physically very able to do so and even though we may know the institution extremely well.

Once admitted to your assigned room, the stripping process continues. It now involves a shedding of clothing. I recall the horror with which a young nurse who happened to have been one of my students looked at me when I informed her that I wanted to remain dressed. I had been admitted for elective surgery, and I knew that there was not much else scheduled for me. I wanted to finish a report which my secretary was to pick up from my room later on. When she asked, "Do you want to wear your own pajamas or would you like a hospital gown?" I said that I would just remain dressed for awhile longer. This young woman became very uncomfortable because, after all, I was an authority figure and she had known me as one of her teachers. I was creating a terrible dilemma because, after all, patients have to take their clothes off so that the hospital can deal with them. And so she did what I have before and since seen nurses do many times. She referred to the fact that the physician might come at any minute and, after all, we would not want to interfere with the physician's work by not being ready for him. The use of one of the other professionals by any of the professionals is a very risky business in offering the patient a sense of teamwork, a sense of confidence, and a sense of inter-professional communications. In order to avoid creating stress, I took my clothes off to make the staff comfortable.

The psychological literature indicates that illness frequently is accompanied by regressive behavior. This is quite correct. However, as a sociologist, I have to raise a word of caution. If we only use this psychological model, it implies that those who care for the sick person stand by his side and merely tolerate the patient's symptoms and hope that the patient will return to mature behavior upon recovery. However, sociologists find that the dependency behavior which patients manifest is no less than a realistic response to the social situation in which they are placed and in which all health profession-als are co-conspirators who must assume shared responsibility.

To add to this point let me suggest that the entire process of admission continues to demonstrate this dependency. Everything that the patient carries has to be surrendered upon admission. This includes even the medications which his own physician has prescribed, has issued, and has trusted the patient to take on his own. These drugs cannot be given again until a new order has been written by the same physician or by someone else. On many occasions time has passed for the next dosage of the medication which stands at the nurse's desk in the patient's own container. But the time passes because no new order has yet been written. This is not only a direct conflict between professional and bureaucratic principles, in which the bureaucratic principles prevail. More importantly, it is a reminder to the patient that the patient's relationship to his or her private physician has been severed and that the hospital as an anonymous agency has become the interloper, the power-wielder, which can withhold from the patient even the drugs prescribed by the patient's own physician. "Is my doctor's word not good anymore? These are the pills that he prescribed for me. Why don't they give them to me? After all, my doctor's name is on the bottle." This undermines not only the confidence in the physician, but it undermines any sense of autonomy which the patient may have left.

Admission also may involve retaking of all those procedures which have previously been undertaken in the physician's office—X-ray, weighing, checking, laboratory tests. If they have been done outside the hospital, they do not count. Bureaucracy will prevail here, too. To quote one patient, "I can accept that they don't trust me, but they don't even seem to trust my doctor."

All of this shapes for the patient two objectives for the hospital stay. The patient arrives in the hospital with the desire and the objective to get well. The new role that is emerging is that "I must survive in the hospital. These are all very powerful people. I must keep myself in good standing in order to get care." This second role aspect competes at times with the objective of getting care. If I have pain and I need something and I know that the nurse might get angry if I turn on that light too frequently, I see myself caught in a power system. One heart patient cradling the signal cord said, "I am saving this button. They appreciate that out there. They know that if I push that button I will really need them fast. They appreciate not having that button used too much."

All of these experiences indicate that patients learn that they must survive effectively within the hospital. In order to do that, they have to find out what the rules of the game seem to be. In schools, students tell each other what they can get away with, what the limits are. Everyone who has ever been with children, as babysitter, knows that the first thing the toddler does with a new sitter is to test the limits. The hospitalized patient also seeks to find out what the rewards and what the punishments are for the behavior within the hospital. However, it is more difficult for the patient to find out, because the rules are not clear, status definitions vary, and there is no informal community of patients. Many a physician and nurse have no idea that their day-to-day behavior with every patient implies rewards and punishments and that they appear to the patient as power figures from the first day that they appear on the patient care unit as students.

Some modern aspects of team nursing need to be looked at from the point of view of patient responses and patient indications. Waiting is punishment. To anticipate the patient's needs is reward. To act as if I do not understand what the patient wants is punishment. The physician who sits down, rewards. The physician who stays far away from the bed, punishes. We asked several physicians to come in and we actually kept track of the time. We asked them to stay in the patient's room for exactly three minutes. Four physicians worked with us on this. With half of the patients, they sat down randomly, and with the other half of the patients, they remained standing a little bit removed from the bed. We then interviewed these patients. Every one of the patients where the physician had sat down thought the physician had stayed at least ten minutes. None of the ones where the physicians remained standing estimated that it was as long.

I recall a fifty-eight year old woman who had been admitted with a cardiac problem, and we interviewed her the next day. The patient said, "You know, when I was admitted, a nurse helped me into my gown. I was sitting down as she was making the bed; she was fastening the signal cord to the pillow, and she told me that if I needed something I should just push the button and the light would go on, and a nurse would come in." This woman smiled at me and continued: "Well, I know how busy these nurses are, so I told her that I hoped I would not have to bother them very much."

Let us examine what this patient did. On one hand she was testing limits. She was saying, "What do you mean? When can I really turn on the signal light?" And secondly, she was scoring points by communicating: "I know you are busy. I appreciate you. I hope you'll appreciate me."

The patient continued in an interview: "You know what this young nurse did? She stopped what she was doing and she came right over to me. She placed her hand on my shoulder and she said that it was none of my concern whether they were busy or not. If I needed something, I should put on the light." If this nurse had continued to be Miss Efficiency of 1962, straightening out the bed and proceeding in her work, she would not have succeeded. To show the patient that if you need something, it's all right to put on the light, she communicated by stepping out of her role. She had the important skill of sensing when to be the official and when to use her informal self, a skill which we sometimes forget. This nurse utilized face-to-face relations, and she used touch.

Patients tend to have a sense of, "I'm entitled to a certain amount of care." This credit depends on the patient's opinion of how sick he is. Less that five percent of the patient population in our study related that claim to service was related to money paid for it. All others indicated consistently that they are entitled to service based on how sick they are.

How do I know how sick I am? The physician does not tell me. The nurses do not tell me. I do not really know. This results in finding ways of determining my service eligibility—of locating the size of my service bank account. The key indicator of the claim to service seems to be the visibility of the claim.

Most visible is the claim of the patient totally strapped to a support frame. He may be scared for his life, concerned about his recovery, but, at least, he has no concerns about his inmate role. Everyone coming in, whether it is a nurse or an aide or a physician, will know that it is legitimate for him to ask for orange juice, water, the urinal, whatever it is. Every drainage bottle, every fluid hanging beside the bed is an increment of the amount of credit. I am not suggesting that the physician order all kinds of bottles just to give patients security. But awareness of the patient's viewpoint is important. This was brought home to me by a patient after a heart attack who before his discharge said, "I never thought that I would ever envy an amputee." I was almost shocked. The patient explained, "When I go home, my doctor will probably tell me that I shouldn't walk up stairs." At that time downtown Chicago had many operator-guided elevators in business buildings with signs which said, "Walk up one flight, walk down two." The patient continued, "If an amputee goes into the elevator, and says 'second floor,' the operator will see the prosthesis and will take him up. What will happen to me? I have no way of legitimizing my going in and asking to be taken up to the second floor. I either have to reveal myself and go through an explanation or I have to walk up. What do you think I'll do? I'll walk up." The peculiar consequence of invisibility of certain conditions becomes a very crucial thing.

The second criterion patients tend to identify is fever. If anyone wants to do a study of the hospital and its status system, one has to consider the caste line between those with temperature and those without. There are rules which indicate that the patient may not be told what his temperature is. Yet, in not telling him how sick he is, we are also not giving him cues to his rights, because as the temperature rises so does the bank account of entitlement to services.

The third thing is pain. It is not as good as visible things because it has to be believed. The patient tries to establish the criteria which determine how much he can ask for. And he gropes for means of organizing his demands. If he can voice demands which the staff seem to approve, then less of his credit is reduced. If he happens to choose a request which appears to meet staff disapproval, then it costs him more.

The patient with an ulcer has been told by his doctor that he should not get upset, that he should not get excited. If he wants something he should ask for it. And he also knows that he is not going to die. Thus he is more likely to ask for things. He is more likely to risk his credit balance than the cardiac patients who say: "I am here without being convinced that everyone knows that I am entitled to complete attention. How do I know when the the nurse's aide comes and does things for me that she agrees that I am entitled to it?" This patient has no visible signs of disability and he also knows that a heart attack can come again. And if it comes, he will need his entire bank account, because speed and good will are crucial, and so he will not try to drain much from his account. If I would give advice to physicians and to nurses, it would be, "Anticipate the need of cardiac patients more than of any other patients."

When we look at the patient's needs and the patient's perception of his own role, we see the patient asking to be told what his rights are so he can understand them better; what rewards and what punishments are in store for him. He would like to be known as an individual and not as number seven hundred thirty-two. He would like to be assured that what is given to him is safe. Happy is the patient who happens to be prescribed a drug that has some psychedelic color scheme, because when it is given to him, at least he knows, "This is my drug." But woe to the patient who receives the indistinguishable white pill. He dares not ask because the nurses would be very stern with him if he does. And yet he's expected to trust the staff that he receives what is intended for him.

This climate of dependence on staff and on the institution drains the patient's sense of uniqueness and of human worth. In this environment it is possible to present one of my *organs* for repair, but it is much more difficult to cope with the fact that *I* am dying. The care I need stems from people's ability to use themselves as deliberate and delicate instruments of help; my organs, however, can respond to the technology and chemistry of medical science.

In summarizing, from the institutional view of the dying process it becomes clear that there are two fundamental issues before us. One is the range of skills, attitudes, and behaviors of the health professions whom we educate to respond to human needs. The other is the organization of a complex social system which we have created to organize these skills and to make available the technological resources of the therapeutic and diagnostic arts. The hospital, it has been suggested, is indeed an institution which has responded admirably to the challenge of healing. It has made possible the division of labor, it has routinized emergencies; but in doing so, it has paid a price and it has reduced, for the sake of human efficiency, the conditions of dignity and of individuality which are part of the human requirement of those who are well, of those who are ill, and of those who are dying.

We have suggested that our professionals have learned to become experts in the management of technological instruments and tools. We have also suggested that in emphasizing instruments and techniques we have diminished their sensitivity and their commitment to their own resources and to their internal strengths. We have not assisted their recognition that being a professional can be as much a helping process as doing the things that professionals do.

I am reminded of an analogy that I should like to offer in conclusion. In our society we have seen the development of the super highway, the interstate network of ribbons of cement which cuts across our country and efficiently and speedily links distant parts of our country with each other. The technological capability of constructing these highways represents the development of maximum efficiency and maximum control over nature by doing away with hills, by filling in valleys, and by bridging streams. When you drive on super highways, you become aware that you have indeed made a choice, and the choice involves gained efficiency of movement, but you have paid the price of feeling that the natural environment has become distant and separated from your immediate proximity. You have paid a price which may have been appropriate. There are times, however, when the experience, the enjoyment, and the need to understand your environment require you to take the sideroad and to seek to commune with nature. The narrow road on which you then choose to travel might appear as a mere reluctant intrusion into the integrity of the world which you seek to understand. This, in a very real way, is the picture of modern patient care. Our hospitals and our health professions have built super highways of medical technology in which the patients' diseases and their organs loom large and where we focus with efficient specificity upon the disease process which we seek to cure. Patient care, however, writes its own script and the dying patient is but one extreme example of the time when the professional challenge demands that we abandon the comfortable road of predictable mileage and dare to venture into the narrow byways which adapt themselves to the individuality of the real world—in this case to the specific needs and human processes of the patient who has entrusted himself to the care of people who could most effectively use themselves as the instruments of help and of hope.

# Death in the First Person

## Anonymous

*In the selection you have just read, Dr. Mauksch asks for a change in hospital
orientation and procedure to accomodate to the human needs for hope, reassurance,
and support from those who care for dying patients. It is unlikely that we will soon
see any policy decisions on an institutional level that will incorporate these
prescriptions into the expected role of professionals on a hospital staff. But it does not
require a policy decision for individuals to change their behavior. As this young nurse
says so eloquently, it doesn't take any more time than you already spend; it's just a
matter of also using that time to minister to the patient's needs as a human being
with hopes and fears and questions and needs for meaningful contact with other
human beings. This piece was published in February, 1970. Its author may have
been dead for several years now. She gave meaning to her life and death through her
reaching out to others with a message that would carry on long after she was gone.
You can further dignify her death if you will receive and act upon this message.*

I am a student nurse. I am dying. I write this to you who are, and
will become, nurses in the hope that by my sharing my feelings with
you, you may someday be better able to help those who share my
experience.

I'm out of the hospital now—perhaps for a month, for six months,
perhaps for a year—but no one likes to talk about such things. In fact,
no one likes to talk about much at all. Nursing must be advancing, but
I wish it would hurry. We're taught not to be overly cheery now, to
omit the "Everything's fine" routine, and we have done pretty well.
But now one is left in a lonely silent void. With the protective "fine,
fine" gone, the staff is left with only their own vulnerability and fear.
The dying patient is not yet seen as a person and thus cannot be

communicated with as such. He is a symbol of what every human fears and what we each know, at least academically, that we too must someday face. What did they say in psychiatric nursing about meeting pathology with pathology to the detriment of both patient and nurse? And there was a lot about knowing one's own feelings before you could help another with his. How true.

But for me, fear is today and dying is now. You slip in and out of my room, give me medications and check my blood pressure. Is it because I am a student nurse, myself, or just a human being, that I sense your fright? And your fears enhance mine. Why are you afraid? I am the one who is dying!

I know you feel insecure, don't know what to say, don't know what to do. But please believe me, if you care, you can't go wrong. Just admit that you care. That is really for what we search. We may ask for why's and wherefore's, but we don't really expect answers. Don't run away—wait—all I want to know is that there will be someone to hold my hand when I need it. I am afraid. Death may get to be a routine to you, but it is new to me. You may not see me as unique, but I've never died before. To me, once is pretty unique!

You whisper about my youth, but when one is dying, is he really so young anymore? I have lots I wish we could talk about. It really would not take much more of your time because you are in here quite a bit anyway.

If only we could be honest, both admit of our fears, touch one another. If you really care, would you lose so much of your valuable professionalism if you even cried with me? Just person to person? Then, it might not be so hard to die—in a hospital—with friends close by.

# 3
# Death through Some Other Windows

In the preceding chapter, we asked the question "Why is it so hard to die?" As an illustration of one of the reasons, we included a selection that described why hospitals do not cope humanely with dying patients. It is routine for people to die in a hospital at this time in this society. But, it is not necessarily best, even though hospitals provide superior *medical* care. Even if hospitals were to reorient their care of the dying to become more humane and supportive in those person's final hours, days, or weeks, nevertheless, hospitals are not home. The most frightening thing about dying for most people is the feeling of being alone, of having to face the unknown without any of the familiar props that usually sustain us in times of great change. Dying in a hospital, as described in the selection you just read, too often includes a stripping away all that is personally defining and meaningful. Dying is hard under any circumstances, but dying in the familiar surroundings of one's home, with those you love and who love you, can take away much of the fear. In this chapter, we will explore some alternatives to death in an institution; we will look through some other windows to see how other cultures provide support and comfort to their dying.

The problem of death is a universal human question. But the answer to that question differs among cultures. In addition to different ways of dealing with those members of the culture who are dying, different human societies have also offered a variety of explanations for the phenomenon of death and its meaning for human existence. And as you will see through comparing the following selections with your own views of death that are a reflection of your own cultural learning, the way that a society or subculture explains death will have a significant impact on the way its members view and experience life. In looking for our own personal answers to the question of death, it is helpful to search beyond the constraints of our own culture to see what other cultures might have to offer that could be useful.

One of my most enlightening experiences in this work has been an intercultural, inter-religious workshop on death and dying in Hawaii, in June of 1970.

We invited representatives of different countries and tried to learn from them how they handled the problems of dying and death in their own environment.

Dr. Frank Mahoney, Associate Professor of Anthropology at the University of Hawaii, shared with us the differences between the American culture and the Micronesian society, the Trukese. While in the United States we have long been known as a death denying society, a people who even deny the aging process itself, the Trukese are regarded as a death affirming society. We are reluctant to reveal our age; we spend fortunes to hide our wrinkles; we prefer to send our old people to nursing homes. For the Trukese, life ends when you are forty; death begins when you are forty.

In that society, you are not regarded as really grown up until you reach the age of forty, until you have the maturity to make decisions and guide your life. This is not an industrial commercial society. In Truk, they rely basically on breadfruit and fish. In order to get fish a young man has to be strong and agile; he has to be a good paddler of a canoe, a good navigator to go out on the reef and gather fish. When the Trukese reaches about forty years of age, his strength begins to decline; he also does not climb trees as well as he used to. And when his strength begins to wane, he begins to feel that his life is ebbing away and he begins to prepare himself for death.

Professor Mahoney related a very moving—and yet so universal— story during this conference, which reinforced my belief that all human beings are basically the same. He told of an old man who—because of a malignancy—was sent from his Island to Hawaii for treatment. He had no one to talk to, no one who understood his language—and worst of all he knew he was dying and wished to be at home with his family. When he was visited by Mahoney, he was able to express his desire, and with strenuous efforts of this friend, he was returned home, where he died two weeks later. He reminds us again and again how difficult it is for us to grapple with institutions. We also have to remember how extraordinarily difficult it is for a human being from an entirely different ethnic and cultural background to get involved in this institutional process. He winds up unable to communicate with anybody in a language that they can understand.

Chief Fuifatu Faulolo, a delightful Samoan High Chief, underlined the need to understand the culture and the customs of the communities in which our patients live and work. Death in Samoa is both hated and feared basically perhaps because they love life and wish to live forever.

Because of their customs they had many troubles with the law during the Vietnam war. When a body of a Samoan soldier was returned from Vietnam for interment in California, the casket was sealed hermetically with clear instructions that it was not to be opened. But one of the Samoan customs requires that they anoint the dead before burial. The members of many a family opened the casket, performed the ritual and then closed the casket again. The families had a very hard time trying to explain their position to the police and the Department of Health there.

Lois Grace, a Deacon of the Kawaiahao Church in Hawaii, shared how her people believe that death is always with them, whether they go fishing, to a party or simply stay at home. Her people are considered superstitious because they strongly believe that Madam Pele was once their goddess and that they will meet all their friends and relatives after death. When someone dies they call in friends and relatives and have a wailing procession, followed by a big luau to pay respect to all those who carried the casket, made the coffin and dug the hole. It helps the one in grief and lightens the burden—and most important of all—it always includes the children, who gather around the casket. It is in this way that children learn early that death is part of life and that difficult times are shared with friends and neighbors in a meaningful community!

Reverend Charles M. C. Kwock spoke on this subject, from the context of Chinese religion, a mixture of Confucianism, Taoism, Buddhism, and nature worship as well as ancestral worship. Chinese are, like their American counterparts, a death denying society. On the other hand they are not only very practical people but they are also quite fatalistic. They believe that death is one of the true certainties in life, that when there is life as a beginning, there is death as an ending.

There is much grief, wailing, and weeping at the time of the funeral. And the Chinese believe in face-saving, in status; if they do not have too many survivors, they even have professional mourners to keep up the status. They believe in life immortality and that the dead live on. They burn paper money in order to give the deceased some money to spend in the other world, and the children used to sell themselves as slaves in order to give their parents a good funeral. At the time of the funeral not only the spirit of the deceased but also other spirits are present. And some of these spirits are not too friendly.

When it is time to cover the casket, they ask the living to turn their backs toward the casket, so that the evil spirits who hover around the dead will not follow them home. To scare the evil spirits, they burn fire crackers at wedding ceremonies especially, so that only good spirits will hover in that auspicious occasion. For the same reason the living would rather have a patient die in a hospital than at home, because the house may be haunted if mother dies at home; to an elderly Chinese the hospital is still associated with the place where you die.

The Japanese too have their rituals, as related by Reverend Yoshiaki Fujitani. For the Japanese, the religion Shintoism is for the living and Buddhism is for the dead. You will therefore find a Shinto shrine and a Buddhist family shrine. When someone dies he goes to the pure land, the other shore, a place often described as beautifully decorated with pools, and silver, gold and lapis lazuli. Death is not something to really fear. Ministers are kept busy with memorial services not especially for the dead, but for the family who wish to remember their dead. They have to observe certain religious practices in order to assure the travel of the spirit to the other world. If the family should neglect to do this, then those spirits return and sort-of "nudge" them.

The rituals include a bed-side service, to give the minister a chance to console the family. The next ceremony is called the Yukan, the bathing of the dead. Nowadays the mortuary does this, but this ritual still lives on in a symbolic form. In the old days the dead could not be kept in the house. The body was thus left outside in the yard. In order to protect it from wild animals, the family stayed up with the dead—this is the origin of the wake service which is done in the mortuary nowadays.

The appreciation service followed the funeral, and because of the long distance that many relatives used to have to travel in old days, food was prepared. When the mourning period was over, a party was given for all the friends and helpers, and it is only then that the family begins to eat meat again.

In modern days, many of these rituals are still maintained; some of them are disappearing. As the American Indians shot arrows up in the air to chase the bad spirits away, the Chinese used noisy firecrackers and others turned their bodies away from the caskets, we—at Arlington Cemetery—shoot a "last salute". With the mobility of the world population, intermarriages between cultures and religions, many younger people are trying to do away with the ceremonials. And yet rituals are a very important part of life. What happens to a second and third generation people when they bury their parents?

Dr. Mahoney responds to that: "We in our family don't really know what to do about it, we may joke about it a little bit. My Japanese wife says: 'you can cremate me, put my ashes in an urn, and paint a big eye on the urn and put it right along side your bed when you go to sleep at night.' "

Rev. Kwock says that in the Chinese situation now, the parents believe in folk religion, the children are Christian. A minister is called to perform a Christian service. In order to satisfy the dead, the elders ask a traditional priest to conduct the funeral service. One is the responsibility toward the dead to carry out their wish, the other toward the living, to give them a comfort in time of grief.

His people believe that everybody born has his destiny already, a time to die according to that destiny. There is a time to get married, according to your destiny, and you find the auspicious day to do those things in order that your life will be harmonized with the universal proper order of things.

Regardless of the particular way that a culture chooses to answer the questions of death, the questions seem to be pretty much the same: what is the meaning of death in human existence? Why do we die when we do, and what happens to us after we die? What relationship is there, if any, between our life here on this earth and our death? Is there a life after death, and if so, what is its nature? Are there ways that we should live our life that will better prepare us for death and the possibility of another life, or is this the only one we get? What is the meaning of human existence? How can we be happy and at peace, and does the answer change if we deny an afterlife? Will we come back to this earth after death, to live another life? If so, does our status in life, our problems and our joys, relate to how we lived our previous lives? Or do we simply die when we die, destined only to rot away and become part of the earth? What is our fortune?

All these questions which have been pondered through history by philosophers, theologians, and common people, can only be answered by speculation; we have no way of knowing the accuracy of our judgments on the issues, and by the time we do know, it will be too late to change the course of our life. It seems most reasonable, therefore, to look for answers that will afford us a sense of peace and strength to live this life with meaning and purpose. I hope the glimpses we offer here through some different windows than those you may ordinarily use to look at death will give you food for thought in answering your own personal questions about death and dying. Whatever you take away from reading these selections, the different perspectives should help you to put your own views into a wider context.

# Dying Among Alaskan
# Indians: A Matter of Choice
## Murray L. Trelease

*In the selection that follows, we hear of the experiences of the author with dying Alaskan Indians. As a priest serving Indian people in villages in the interior of Alaska, the author was regularly called to pray for dying old people and to bring Communion. What was unusual about this experience was that in nearly every case, the dying people exhibited a willfulness about their death, their participation in its planning, and the time of its occurrence that showed a remarkable power of personal choice. This experience is in sharp contrast to our traditional belief that death comes like a thief in the night, unexpected, and unprepared for. The importance of this selection is to remind us of the necessity of human beings' taking an active role in all aspects of their lives, even their own dying and death. The descriptions of dying and all that surrounded the deaths of these Alaskan Indians suggest that the end of life can be meaningful and growth-producing. There is much in their rituals that we could borrow to bring meaning to death in our society.*

In the 1960's, I spent eight years serving small Indian villages in the interior of Alaska as a parish priest. The people I served, before the coming of white men and western civilization, had been nomadic, traveling in small family groups to hunt and fish. With the coming of the white man, a rapid evolution took place from nomadic families to village communities. But it was not an even evolution and the attitudes and values of nomadic life survived long after people had settled in villages. People who had been raised in the old way of life, if not actually nomadic, were at least heavily imbued with the customs and values of that life. It is those customs and values, in their relationship to death and dying, that I wish to describe.

33

During the period that I spent in Alaska, I had some very unusual experiences with death and dying that I would like to share with you. A young member of a family would come to my cabin and ask me to come pray for grandma and bring Communion. And when I arrived the whole family and close friends would be there and we would have a service together. Within hours after that, the person would be dead. Sometimes the summons would originate with a member of the family and, occasionally, with a nurse stationed in a larger village. But most often it was the one dying who called everyone together. And I was told on several occasions that the dying person had spent the past few days making plans, telling the story of his life and praying for all the members of the family. There were as many variations on the theme as there were personalities. Some liked to have a lot of people with them and others preferred just a favorite relative or to be alone. On several occasions when taking Christmas or Easter Communions to the shut-ins, the old man or woman would tell me that he had been waiting for me. And death would occur soon after they had received the sacrament. I do not suggest that everyone waited for the priest to come and then died right away. But the majority who did not die suddenly did some degree of planning, had some kind of formal service or celebration of prayers and hymns and farewells.

By far the most dramatic instance of timing and planning was the dying of Old Sarah. About two weeks before her death I received a radio message from Old Sarah summoning me to Arctic Village on a specific day. Nothing like this had happened to me before but I can remember thinking "she intends to die on that day." Dutifully I gathered three of her family in Fort Yukon and flew them to Arctic Village on the day designated. I was right about her intentions but wrong about the date. She had a son in another village and wished me to go and bring him to Arctic Village. She allowed enough time for me to bring in the last person. It was quite a company of people as was fitting for the undisputed matriarch of both the family and the community.

During the morning of the next day she prayed for all the members of her family. At noon we had a great celebration of the Eucharist in her cabin complete with all the hymns and prayers. Old Sarah loved every minute of it, joined in the prayers and the singing and was quite bright throughout the service. Then we all left and at six in the evening she died. For the next two days the entire village turned out on the business of Sarah's funeral. Some of the women prepared her body and completely cleaned her cabin while others cooked vast quantities of food, much of which Sarah had bought for the occasion, for the workers. The mission house was turned into a carpentry shop for making the coffin and teams of men took turns picking and shoveling a grave in the frozen ground. All the village packed into the church for the service and accompanied the coffin to the graveyard, ' singing hymns while the grave was filled in with dirt and placing hand-made crepe paper flowers on the mound before the final blessing. Then there was a great feast for all the village. The burial customs were similar to these in all the villages but never before or since in my experience were they planned and shared so much by the one who died. Old Sarah's dying was a priceless gift to all of us.

Because these experiences were with the old I wondered often how much of the acceptance of death and awareness of dying came from pre-Christian days. No one seemed to know about that. But there were legends about the spirit world and life after death. The pre-Christian religion was a form of animism. And the spirits of which people were aware were either evil and harmful or, at best, mischievous and capricious. The spirits of evil animals, like the wolverines, were placated and bribed after death to keep them from harming the living, spoiling the hunting, or haunting a camp. If there were any good spirits, they were known because they didn't bother anyone. One legend I heard had it that the spirits of evil people went a little distance (from the Fort Yukon area) to the head of a stream known appropriately as Preacher Creek. They were thought to come into the camps of the people and haunt or cause trouble. The spirits of good people, on the other hand, went down the Yukon River and were never heard from again. Whether there was any idea of life or a place after death for them I never heard.

With the coming of the Christian gospel the people were introduced for the first time to a good spirit, the Holy Spirit. His greater power and his love for his people was "Good News" indeed. But in addition to confidence in the Holy Spirit, there was for many old people I knew a very warm, personal relationship with Jesus. One old man used to tell me about his conversations with Jesus at night. He was one of the people I sought out when my well "went dry." And he and most of the others understood that death was the beginning of a close and never ending life with Jesus. The children of people who died told me on many occasions that the parting words of their parents were filled with testimony and teaching about Jesus. That sort of witness answered for me the question of whether these people had a positive anticipation of death. But the other question—how they determined when life should end—was never answered. Perhaps no one could have put it into words. It did seem obvious, however, that each one of these individuals sensed, perhaps intuitively, that meaningful life was drawing to a close and was able to enter the final phase easily and naturally. Certainly few of them required the services of a doctor to tell them they were terminal.

I do not want to suggest that there is some super-human quality about human volition. But my Alaskan experiences and other experiences with the dying to the present day affirm my conviction that it is a powerful and sometimes determinative factor in dying. It does not seem strange to believe this considering that it is powerful and determinative throughout the rest of life. It is not that human will changes reality but rather that it is a part of the reality of life and needs to be reckoned with.

From a pastor's point of view it is less important to define and measure volition than it is to understand what it means to an individual to have a will and how it may be supported and liberated. All too often families and pastors and even medical staff assume that all a dying person wants is to be comfortable. Once the death sentence is passed, we tend to fluff up the pillows and hope, for his or her sake, that death will come soon. We are terribly anxious about pain and seek the latest medications, most of which deaden the mind as well as the body. I am not prepared to say that this is all wrong. But I do believe we have our priorities confused. Someone's life is about to end. Surely, there are important things for that person to say and do before he dies!

Of course the prime responsibility for living out this last phase is with the individual himself. Others may influence and support his will, but only he can exercise it. One of the important things I learned in Alaska was to ask a dying person "What do you want?" It is not a question of comfort but of mental activity and moral choice. "Would you like to see your son (whom you haven't spoken to for 10 years)?" "Is there someplace you would like to go or something you would like to do?" "Would you like to give someone a gift?" Of course the questions don't come out like that, and of course one is aware of physical and mental limitations. But the point is that dying should be seen as a phase of living and subject to growth and obligations and opportunities just as is every other phase of living.

I remember a nineteen year old boy dying of leukemia who in two weeks' time grew from a rather irresponsible brat to a loving, understanding counselor who led his family through the shattering experience of his dying. When he first learned he was dying he could think of nothing but rejection and resentment. But a short time later he discovered that he had a long agenda of things he wanted to know and understand. There were people to see, old sores to heal, his family to help and comfort; he was still thinking of more things to accomplish when he died suddenly. Not everyone will want all those things. But unfortunately too many people think that the sentence of death, rather than death itself, is an end to growth. On the contrary, it may mark the beginning of the greatest growth of a lifetime in understanding, love, and faith.

If I have succeeded in making the point about active volition in dying, then I have only to add that we as the community—family, friends, pastors, doctors and nurses—often hold the key to the liberation of the dying person's will. Old Sarah didn't need much bolstering of her will. She was on familiar ground with familiar people and was carrying out a long tradition. But in our communities today many people die in some kind of isolation; a strange hospital room, the regimen of hospital life, controlled visits, medication (often mind-dulling) and possibly a battery of life-support systems. How can an individual exert much will, continue growing and reaching out, and giving in that kind of setting? That defines the task of those who love him: to break through the isolation and offer human warmth, the liveliness of one personality in contact with another and the opportunity for the dying to be heard and understood and to give his gifts of love.

# The Jewish View of Death:
# Guidelines for Dying

## Rabbi Zachary I. Heller

*In the preceding selection we saw how individuals of the nomadic Alaskan Indian culture drew upon their own customs and their communities' resources to make their deaths personally meaningful. In the selection that follows, the author explains the rituals of the Jewish culture, set down in Jewish law, which provide for death with dignity and meaning—allowing the dying person to set his house in order, bless his family, pass on any messages to them he feels important, and make his peace with God. The meaningfulness with which these dictates of Jewish law are carried out, as in any situation, depends on the persons participating in the rituals as well as the degree to which the dying person's Jewish identity is integrated into his total life. But the prescribed procedures accompanying the dying of an individual of the Jewish faith and culture, if followed with meaning, give an outlet to the needs of the dying person.*

Human mortality may not be denied, for death is the common end to all life. To the individual of traditional faith, death is not an end but a transition from one state of human existence to another. Yet, while we may be willing to accept the ultimate effect of this transition with equanimity, the process of dying is fraught with many anxieties that cannot be easily resolved. It is of course a truism that death is part of the natural order and must be accepted as such, but its denial is often a major emotional problem for the subject, the family concerned, and even the physician. What must be comprehended by all is that this element of life's circumstances is inevitable, although at times it may be postponed temporarily.

Contemporary social literature has witnessed a tremendous increase in writing about death and dying. Dr. Elisabeth Kübler-Ross's

---

pioneering work in this field, *On Death and Dying* (1969) analyzes five stages of reaction on the part of the terminally ill patient. They are: 1) denial and isolation 2) anger 3) bargaining 4) depression and 5) acceptance. Whereas these reactions do not always occur in this full sequence, they constitute the typical spectrum of emotional response. These psychological insights into the emotions of the dying patient have now further sensitized attending medical personnel to the human needs of the patient who wants to be treated not as a clinical specimen but as a person.

This emergent concern with the emotional welfare of the terminally ill is, by contrast, not new to Judaism. We are mandated to make certain that this last period of life be as anxiety-free as possible. However, a tension does exist between this ideal and the need for realistic acceptance of death and preparation for it.

It has been noted that only a minority of people today die in the familiar surroundings of their homes or place of occupation. We usually automatically remove the terminally ill to the sterile atmosphere of the medical center. Consequently, the dying patient is estranged from the emotional security of the family and the familiar at the point of greatest emotional trauma. In fact, death itself is usually referred to only euphemistically in major segments of our society, and children are shielded from knowledge of it, as if it were some unnatural and immoral act. Many of our contemporary attitudes toward the dying and funeral practices after death seek to negate the naturalness of this element in the life cycle. On the other hand, Jewish tradition confronts death directly and specifically views the period of terminal illness *("Shechiv Mera")* and dying *("Goses")* as a time when loved ones should surround, comfort, and encourage the patient.

Family and physician often face the dilemma of communicating the nature and severity of illness to a terminal patient. Psychiatrists present varying perspectives which take into account the patient's ability and desire to cope with and accept such information. Two Biblical precedents are often cited as the basis for Jewish insights into this problem. Both narratives are found in *II Kings*. In chapter 8, Ben Hadad, the Syrian King, asks his aide, Hazazl, to inquire of the prophet Elisha about his chances for recovery from illness. Elisha responds to him: "Go, say to him—'You shall certainly recover' but the Lord has showed me that he shall surely die." Following this example, the Rabbis urge withholding information about the severity of illness and rather attempting to give the patient hope in possible recovery. In the twentieth chapter of *II Kings*, however, we find another precedent which is at variance with the first one.

In those days Hezehiah became sick so that he was near to death. Isaiah the prophet the son of Amoz came to him and said: "Thus says the Lord, 'Set your house in order for you shall die and shall not live.' "

A later Rabbinic opinion cited in the Midrash chastises the prophet for removing all hope for possible recovery. In fact, however, the *Hallacha* (the Jewish legal system) structures a framework for informing the terminal patient of the severity of his condition, yet at the same time, making allowance for keeping some spark of hope alive.

The terminally ill is to be encouraged to put both his temporal and spiritual affairs in order. "One tells him to set his mind on his affairs, . . . but let this not cause him to be afraid of death." (Yoreh Deah 335:7)

In fact, some sources indicate that the patient is to be reassured with the counsel: "For words can cause neither life nor death." (Bet Yosef)

The deathbed confessional is viewed as an important element in the transition to the world to come. The dying patient is to be instructed to recite the confessional according to the limitations of his physical and mental condition. "And one says (to the patient), 'Many have confessed and have not died and many who have not confessed have died, as a reward for your confession you will live, and whoever confesses has a portion in the world to come.' " (Yoreh Deah 378:1)

This deathbed scene is thus structured to give the terminally ill and dying patient an outlet for expression of natural concerns and anxieties, yet within a reassuring framework which never attempts to be deluding.

Solomon Schechter suggests that the Rabbinic concept of *Teshuvah* —repentance—which is the essence of the deathbed confessional, is a means of reconciliation with God. The confessional would be, therefore, comforting rather than distressing. The basic formula of the confessional has a reassuring quality.

I acknowledge before you Lord My God and God of my fathers that both my healing and my death are in your hands. May it be Your will to heal me in a complete recovery. If, though, I do die, may my death atone for all my sins and transgressions that I have committed before you. Grant me a share in the world to come. . . .

The terminal patient is thus urged to face the future realistically with death as a real and perhaps imminent possibility. The *hallacha* simplifies the legal process of deathbed testaments. It modifies the requirements for witnesses and accepts oral dispositions as having validity equal to a properly executed written document.

Another aspect of this issue is the confrontation of the family not with the distribution of material possessions but with ethical instruction. The Bible again provides the earliest source of this tradition. The Patriarch Isaac, recognizing that his days are numbered, calls his first born to him. He charges Esau, "So that I may give you my blessing before I die." (*Gen.* 27) Joseph took his two sons Ephraim and Menassah to the bedside of grandfather Jacob so that they might receive his blessing. Jacob then called his twelve sons to him and pronounced his ethical will. Innumerable parents throughout the ages have similarly instructed their children regarding family unity, loyalty to religious traditions and ethical imperatives before they died.

Each of these procedures—repentance, confession, the ordering of one's material affairs, the blessing of family, and ethical instruction— takes into account the theological, practical and emotional needs of the terminal patient. They enable the patient to express fears, find comfort and inner strength, and communicate meaningfully with those close to him.

The second area of concern relates to the inevitability of death as a natural phenomenon and possible human involvement or intervention in it. What is our moral responsibility to prolong life and when shall we feel free to permit the angel of death to carry out its task?

Recent spectacular advances in medical science and technology do not always produce unmixed blessings. The medical profession has placed great emphasis upon preserving life almost at any cost. It has been noted by numerous writers in this field that the death of the patient in a way may be seen as the failure of the medical art and its practitioner. We must keep in mind the realization "that the attitudes and techniques developed in the battle against untimely death may not be entirely appropriate in helping the aged patient adapt to changed physiological and psychological circumstances." (Dr. Robert S. Morison, *Scientific American*, September, 1973, p. 55) The moral dilemma facing physician and family often involves the acceptance of death as the natural outcome of events. When life has been extended through preventative and curative medicine to a point where the chronic deteriorations of old age or the ravages of disease have taken their toll, the physician must be willing to cease and desist. It is then our human task to keep the dying patient as comfortable as possible while nature follows its eternal course.

We often hear the phrase "death with dignity" sounded as the rallying cry for those who propose active or passive forms of euthanasia. It is clear that *"hallacha"* views active euthanasia as outright murder. Hastening the patient's demise through any act of willful commission is definitely forbidden. The halachic distinction between the two stages of "terminal illness" and "dying," as referred to above, must again be called to the reader's attention. During the first phase all efforts, no matter how extraordinary, must be made to support life and prolong it. The situation varies somewhat in the second and final phase. That mandate is not clear cut. The glosses of Isserles to the Shulchan Aruch specifically state that—

"if there is some exterior force preventing the expiration of life (lit. the exit of the soul from the body) it is permitted to remove it."

Thus the issue must be resolved as to whether the removal of extraordinary measures that support the physical life systems mechanically might thus be permitted in the case of the dying patient. Rabbi Immanuel Jakobovits suggests in his study *Jewish Medical Ethics* that such action might be halachically acceptable.

"Jewish law sanctions, and perhaps even demands, the withdrawal of any factor—whether extraneous to the patient himself or not—which may artificially delay his demise in the final phase. It might be argued that this modification implies the legality of expediting the death of an incurable patient in acute agony by withholding from him such medicaments as sustain his continued life by unnatural means—an issue also considered in Catholic moral philosophy. Our sources refer only to cases in which death is expected to be imminent; it is, therefore, not altogether clear whether they would tolerate this moderate form of euthanasia, though that cannot be ruled out." (pp. 123-4)

The Hassidic Master, Rabbi Nahman of Bratizlav is reported to have commented that "the dead must be amused when people bewail him, as if to say: it would have been better if you had lived longer and suffered more." He expresses the sensitive understanding that we neither hallow life nor do the suffering patient any favor by prolonging the pain and anguish that are often part of the throes of death. The death of Moses is represented in the Jewish tradition as the ideal death. He expired as if with a kiss. As a divine gift he was spared the agony of dying. It seems to be well within the letter and spirit of

*Hallacha* that physician and family seek to alleviate the physical pain and emotional distress of the dying patient by some acts of omission, especially removal of heroic measures utilizing mechanical life support systems.

It is axiomatic that each case must be judged independently, taking into account objective medical judgements and the subjective considerations of the patient's physical and emotional condition and needs. As Dr. Robert Morison has noted, "Medicine can fend off death, but in doing so it often merely prolongs agony." (op. cit.) Science and the technology it has produced are no longer "value free," absolved of facing the moral dilemmas and decisions that must guide their practical application to the human situation. These judgments must be made within the framework of a system of moral philosophy which views not only the immediate situational ethic but the long range ramifications as well. The Jewish tradition has long considered the principles underlying these issues.

Contemporary programs to alleviate the distress of terminally ill and dying patients are very much in consonance with teachings of the Jewish tradition which stress the normalcy of these events of the life cycle. The patient's emotional equilibrium is maintained, with the continued support of family and community, who perform the mitzvah of "Bikkur Cholim"—visiting the sick with a sensitivity nurtured by their religious tradition. When death, the natural end of human existence, inevitably does come it is accepted as the decree of human mortality by the Eternal and Righteous Judge.

# The Jewish View of Death: Guidelines for Mourning

## Audrey Gordon

*The previous selection explained the ways in which Jewish law and tradition provide humane guidelines to help the dying Jew find comfort, peace, and opportunity for resolution of unfinished business and communication with loved ones. This selection takes us beyond the death and describes the processes set forth in Jewish law and tradition to provide a structure through which the loved ones of the dead person can mourn his loss and become reintegrated into the community of life.*

*I hope that these two papers by Jewish scholars help our non-Jewish readers involved with dying patients to appreciate, understand and perhaps be less evasive when we enter a room of a patient of another religious background. We may find in this philosophy of a people with so long a history of cohesive faith, some humane guidelines, whatever our religion, for defining and meeting the needs both of those who are dying and of those who are mourning the loss of a loved one who has died.*

The concept of wisdom (Chockmah) in the Bible is not that of sage philosophy or metaphysical abstraction. Wisdom in the Bible means doing what is right in each situation. It is in this sense that the Jewish perspectives on death and the Jewish mourning practices are "wise". They are wise because they provide a total framework within which man learns to accept death, to mourn completely, and to live again fully.

When the family and community are faced with the prospect of the death of one of its members, Jewish law reminds us that "a dying man is considered the same as a living man in every respect." [1] But in American culture today, dying is treated as if it were a separate realm of existence. America is essentially a death-denying society; consequently we treat the dying differently than we do the living. We avoid

---

Originally titled "The Psychological Wisdom of the Law," from *Jewish Reflections on Death*, ed. Jack Riemer. Copyright © 1974 by Schocken Books, Inc.
[1] Dov Zlotnick, *The Tractate: Mourning*, Yale Judaica Series, Vol. XVII, New Haven, Conn., 1966, page 31.

them, or avoid honest communication with them. We try to spare them the problems of everyday living, and we thereby deprive them of its joys. The dying person lives alone in an artificial environment, created by those who do not wish to cope with the fact of death and its inevitable call to every living being.

*Hallacha* forbids this dishonest approach. The dying person must be treated as he was always treated, as a complete person capable of conducting his own affairs and able to enter fully into human relations even unto death. Further, the Jewish tradition of never leaving the bedside of the dying is of immense value, not only to the dying person but also to those about to be bereaved. How helpless and how guilty we must feel when we hear of the death of a loved one, especially if no one was there to ease the fear of uncertainty and the pain of separation. All kinds of questions spring to mind from the wellsprings of guilt: "Was everything done that could have been done?" "Why didn't the doctor or nurse get there sooner?" "What could I have done to prevent this?" "Did he suffer?" "Why was he alone?" And underneath these questions lie another series of questions: "Will I suffer?" "Will I be alone?" "Will anyone care for me though I didn't care for him?" Judaism shields mourners from being overwhelmed by this kind of guilt because the community shares in the care of the dying so that they are never left alone. The community provides reassurances that everything appropriate was done. To the extent that I am a part of the community part of me *was* there when he died and so I need not be afraid.

The bedside vigil serves one more purpose. As death approaches, a crisis of faith occurs as the life-cycle draws to an end. A personal confessional is encouraged from the dying as a *rite de passage* to another phase of existence. This type of confessional occurs throughout the Jewish life cycle whenever one stage has been completed. So we confess on the Day of Atonement as we end one year of life and begin another. So brides and grooms traditionally said the confessional and fasted on their wedding day for they sensed that it marked the end of one stage in their lives and the beginning of another. The confessional on the death-bed is the recognition of the ending of one cycle and the beginning of another. This together with the recitation of the *Shema* in the last moments before death helps to affirm faith in God precisely when it is most challenged and helps the dying person focus on those most familiar rituals of his life just at the moment when he enters the most mysterious and unknowable experience of his life. This comforts him together with those who share his vigil.

The wisdom in actually observing the death is that the reality can then not be denied. Psychiatrists know that the relatives of those missing in action or those who are lost in battle and whose bodies are never recovered have the hardest time recuperating from grief for they have no body around on which to focus and express their grief and they are vulnerable to the temptation to deny the reality of the death. Judaism does not permit the mourner to escape the reality of death and so bids him see it and then leads him through a whole network of burial and mourning procedures to help him come to terms with death. This is in harmony with psychiatric literature which abounds with examples of the fearful consequences of death-denial and repression of grief. The Talmudic sages centuries ago seem to have sensed the same truth that psychiatrists now articulate, which is that "the recognition of death is a necessity for continuing life (and grief), is a necessary process in normative psychological functioning." [2]

When death occurs, Jewish law demands that immediate plans be made for burial. This is in accord with the ancient belief that it was a great dishonor and disrespect not to inter the dead. Making funeral plans serves as a necessary activity for the mourner at the beginning of the grief process. The mourner reaffirms his concern for the dead through actions which serve at the same time to overcome his wish for identification and incorporation with the lost loved one. The *onen* through his actions knows that he is "not dead," not still and lifeless, as he may consciously or unconsciously feel or wish himself to be.

During this first period of grief there is an intense desire on the part of the bereaved to do whatever he can for the dead. Jewish tradition meets this need by placing the responsibility for all the funeral arrangements upon the mourner, not by shielding and excusing him from these tasks. It even releases the *onen* from the obligation to perform any positive religious commandments, which on all the other days of his life are binding, so that he may devote himself instead to those burial preparations and arrangements. [3]

A funeral according to *Hallacha* emphasizes that death is death. Realism and simplicity are the characteristics of the Jewish burial. In this respect it stands in clear contrast to the American funeral ritual which, as Dr. Vivian Rakoff has said, "is constructed in such a way as to deny all its most obvious implications." [4] The modern American

---

[2] Vivian M. Rakoff, "Psychiatric Aspects of Death in America", in *Death in American Experience*, Schocken Books, New York, N.Y. 1974, p. 159.
[3] Shubert, Spero, *Journey into Light: A Manual for the Mourner*. The Spero Foundation, 1959, p. 22.
[4] Rakoff, op. cit. p. 158.

customs such as viewing the body, cosmetics, elaborate pillowed and satined coffins, and green artificial carpeting that shields the mourners from seeing the raw earth of the grave are all ways in which the culture enables us to avoid confronting the reality of death. Other associated practices such as sedating the mourners, hurrying them away from the grave, and keeping children away from the cemetery are part of the same pattern and are to be deplored. They only serve to reinforce feelings of unreality: "This isn't really happening" or "he isn't really dead." Whenever American Jews adopt such customs they cheat themselves of the valuable and healing grief work built into the Jewish funeral. "The disservice that the funeral parlor's denial of death does to the surviving families should continue to be publicized and the rightness of expressing grief in passionate form encouraged." [5]

The simplicity of the Jewish burial averts another psychological pitfall. The religious prescription for plain unadorned simple coffins and for the avoidance of ostentation in the funeral itself serves as a deterrent to the excessive expenditure of family funds for irrational reasons. This expense is often the way that the family represses its guilt over past treatment of the dead or defends itself against its feelings of anger because the loved one has abandoned them. These feelings need to be worked through as a normal part of the process of grief so that later the memories of the deceased can be enjoyed without pain or avoidance. The working through of ambivalent feelings toward the dead by members of the family is extremely important in order to avoid later psychosomatic damage.[6]

I have myself conducted therapeutic interviews with such people, suffering from various forms of cancer and ulcerative colitis, in which the onset of the disease could be traced to a time shortly after a

---

[5] Rakoff, *Ibid*, p. 160.

I am not suggesting that when these practices are specifically requested by the family that the funeral director should ignore them, only that the family should be educated in the Jewish funeral tradition. It has been my experience that funeral directors are more than willing to conduct a funeral in the spirit and form of the Jewish tradition if the family so wishes.

[6] "In acute grief the element of guilt is invariably present. This is probably due to the ambivalent quality in the love relationship where there is self-giving and self-satisfying at the same time, a craving for mutuality between the lover and the beloved, as well as the resentment at the loss of freedom that love inevitably entails. When the love object dies the feelings are set free and there is guilt." Edgar Jackson, "Grief and Religion" in *Death In American Experience*, op. cit. p. 223. The seminal article on this continues to be Dr. Erich Lindemann's "Symptomology and Management of Acute Grief," *American Journal of Psychiatry*, 101, September, 1944, in which Dr. Lindemann discusses his findings in treating the bereaved survivors of the Coconut Grove fire in Boston, Mass. This study really broke new ground and created interest in the scientific study of grief reactions and death attitudes.

traumatic loss that had somehow not been fully faced up to and resolved. In each case the patient displayed ambivalence and unresolved grief. For example, a woman in her late sixties was admitted to the hospital with severe abdominal pains for which no physiological cause could be found. A preliminary psychiatric consultation indicated that she was severely depressed but assumed that it was simply because of her advancing age and her excessive dependency needs. But my conversation with her elicited the fact that she had not attended the funeral of her daughter who had died of cancer four years before. She had never confronted the reality of her daughter's death, and she felt somehow that God was punishing her because she had not gone to the funeral. Her pain now was (in her mind) His punishment for what she had not done then. When we began the grief work and she spilled forth her guilt and her anger at her daughter for leaving her by dying, her physical symptoms began to subside and she was soon able to return home. She was still in some pain but it was now recognized for what it was, emotional pain, and therapy became helpful. Her rabbi agreed to help her continue working through her long delayed expression of grief.

In a much more tragic case, a twenty-eight year old man refused to permit a life saving operation to be performed on him in order to stop the spread of his cancer. His two-year-old only son had died just three months before of leukemia and the father's grief was so overwhelming and unresolved and his identification with his son was so complete that he no longer wished to live. His family could not dissuade him and he died soon after.

"The most striking Jewish expression of grief is the rending of garments by the mourner prior to the funeral service. The rending is an opportunity for psychological relief. It allows the mourner to give vent to his pent-up anger and anguish by means of a controlled, religiously sanctioned, act of destruction." [7]

*Kriyah*, the tearing of clothes, is a visible dramatic symbol of the internal tearing asunder that the mourner feels in his relationship with the deceased. Even after the *shivah* is over, the garments may never be completely mended but must show the external scar of the internally healing wound. Reminders such as these constantly elicit grief reactions even as the mourner slowly begins to take up the patterns of everyday living.

---

[7] Maurice Lamn, *The Jewish Way In Death and Mourning*, Jonathan David Pub. Co., New York, N.Y., 1969, page 38.

Judaism opposes repression of the emotions and enjoins the mourner to express his grief and sorrow openly. In the funeral itself there are several signals for the full outpouring of grief. The eulogy is intended to make the mourner aware of what he has lost. Traditionally its function was to awaken tears. The familiar pattern of prayer now has a heart-rending newness, as the *El Maley Rachamim*, heard so many times before, is recited this time with the name of the dead for the first time. At the cemetery the recitation of the *Kaddish* stirs the memories of all who have mourned, and they join in collective sorrow together with the newly bereaved to affirm God's will and glory.

The saying of the *Kaddish* is such an important part of the grieving process that women as well as men should be allowed to participate in it on an equal basis. The Women's Liberation movement has raised our consciousness and made us more sensitive to the deprivation of women from religious experiences which was unconscious and unintentional for so long. One of the first to understand it and respond to it was Henrietta Szold, the famous founder of Hadassah. In 1916 she wrote a letter to Hayim Peretz thanking him for his offer to say Kaddish for her and her sisters when their mother died. She points out that it was the tradition in her family for the daughters to perform this responsibility in the absence of sons and that she believes the Kaddish was never intended to be a duty for males only.

Henrietta Szold's affirmation of woman's rights and woman's needs in the time of mourning, written more than a half century before the current movement for woman's place of equality, should be a model for all modern Jews.

The raw gaping hole in the earth, open to receive the coffin, symbolizes the raw emptiness of the mourner at this moment of final separation. Burying the dead by actually doing some of the shoveling themselves helps the mourners and the mourning community to ease the pain of parting by performing one last act of love and concern. What more familial and poignant act is there than that of "putting to rest" as children are put to rest at night by their parents. I have seen mourners standing simply transfixed as cemetery workers callously filled in the hole until they could bear it no more and tore the shovels from their hands to finish the burial themselves.

When the burial is completed the grief work intensifies as the focus of the community's concern shifts to the mourner. "Mourning is essentially a process of unlearning the expected presence of the deceased." [8] Returning from the cemetery the mourner finds a "meal

---

[8] Rakoff, op. cit. p. 159.

of recuperation" waiting for him. The meal serves several purposes. First, it is a visible sign of communal solidarity reassuring the mourner that he is not alone and that others stand ready to help him even if the one who helped him in life until now is gone. Second, it restates the theme of life and forces the mourner to recognize that his life must still go on, even though he may feel now that it too has ended with the loss of his loved one. The first mandatory meal is a resocializing and an "unlearning" experience. Until now the mourner was allowed to withdraw into his own pain and loss and identification with the deceased, but now the community reaches out to redirect him back towards the path of complete living.

With that first meal there begins the week of *shivah*, the institution through which the tradition advances the grief work for the mourner most effectively. Grief work begins with the initial release of feelings usually expressed in the recounting of the events that led up to the death, and moves from there to the recounting of the memories of the life. Edgar Jackson, writing outside the Jewish tradition, speaks unknowingly in terms that parallel the *shivah* experience when he says: "It is important that the bereaved person have a safe framework within which he can express all the feelings that are set in motion within him by the loss of the beloved. It is also important that the means of expression meet the needs of the psyche. The ritualized religious expression does this by releasing the emotional responses that grow from group memory and group support, that justify and accept deep feelings of pain without requiring explanations, all at a level below the threshold of consciousness." [9]

The *shivah* brings the mourners together to retell and relive their experiences of the death and to share once again the memories from the past when the family circle was whole. The condolence call provides the mourner with the opportunity to tell his story many different times to many different people, each of whom are enjoined to allow the mourner to speak first so that his interests are allowed to be the focus of conversation. The visitor is not asked to say platitudes, but only to listen and by listening to enable the griever to vent his feelings. If a mourner cannot find the words with which to express his grief, then the comforter comforts him with his silence and with his shared physical presence. At a time when there are no words, the comforter should feel no need to fill the air with chatter or to divert the mourner. Silence has its own kind of eloquence and sometimes it can be more precious than words.

---

[9] Jackson, op. cit. p. 224.

Judaism recognizes that there are levels and stages of grief and so it organizes the year of mourning into three days of deep grief, seven days of mourning, thirty days of gradual readjustment, and eleven months of remembrance and healing. Thus the mourner is drawn forth from his temporary isolation to increasingly larger personal and communal responsibilities and involvements until by the end of the year he has been reintegrated into the community and his loss has been accepted, though not forgotten.

There are many customs and traditions of mourning within Judaism. Some of them are actually *Hallacha*, others are simply customs and accretions that have attached themselves to the tradition down through the centuries. Whatever their origins, these traditions serve well the families who use them primarily as a means of expressing their loss and accepting their bereavement. The intention of all mourning practices should be the fullest possible outpouring of grief and the opportunity for the family and the community to reknit after the loss of one of its members so that they may continue to be able to love and to work. "The expression of feeling is not designed to lead to despair and to separation from the community but rather to make legitimate and more easily possible a return and a reinvestment of emotional capital in the next chapters of life." [10]

The Jewish tradition, seasoned by centuries of experience in suffering and surviving, provides a network of ways in which to affirm life in the face of death. It is a tradition that contains the wisdom which enables us to express our grief, to strengthen our family and community ties, to honor God, and to accept His will.

> "On the day when death will knock at thy door
>     What wilt thou offer him?
> I will set before my guest the full vessel of my life.
>     I will never let him go with empty hands. . . .
>                                                   Rabindranath Tagore

---

[10] Jackson, op. cit., p. 231.

# The Death That Ends Death
# in Hinduism and Buddhism

## J. Bruce Long, Ph.D.

*The preceding selections in this chapter dealt mainly with ways of dying in different cultural settings—attitudes and rituals surrounding death. This piece, by contrast, is a more purely philosophical view of the meaning of death in human existence. It is a particularly fascinating historical account of the development of a philosophy of life and death in a culture whose general development has differed in many ways from our own. At a time of increased interest in Eastern religion and philosophy, not as a substitute for our more familiar ideas, but rather as a source of complementary ideas to be integrated with our own, this selection should provide you with much food for thought. Some of you may find in the descriptions of death and afterlife as it relates to life here on this earth a more comforting explanation of the relationship between life and death than that offered in many Western religions. All of you should find it an interesting contrast to our current Western tendency to dissociate death from life.*

One of the most ironic facts about the present age is that, at a time when efforts of heroic proportions are being expended on all sides to discover the means either to conquer death or to postpone its arrival as long as possible, there should occur such a pervasive preoccupation with the subject of death as has appeared in contemporary literature, journalism, television, and cinema. It is as though modern man had reached a consensus that he might reduce death to a harmless nonentity merely by writing and talking about it to the point of exhaustion.

There are, at least, two images of death which seem to inform a large proportion of contemporary fiction, drama and cinema. On the

---

one hand, death is pictured as an ancient enemy who, after centuries of fruitless struggle, is being brought under submission by man's scientific and technological ingenuity. Second, death is imagined as a chilling wind, blowing wherever it wills to snuff out the flame of life in anyone who gets in its way, leaving for those who remain behind only a sense that life is an inexhaustible draught of ennui or anxiety.

This latter vision of death as total annihilation, devoid of any sign of redemptive purpose, is presented in provocative terms by one of the two leading characters of Tom Stoppard's drama, *Rosencrantz and Guilderstern Are Dead*. Guilderstern comments upon the anticipation of his own death with painful irony: "No, no. It's not like that. Death isn't romantic . . . death is not anything . . . death is . . . not. It's the absence of presence, nothing more . . . the endless time of never coming back. . . . A gap you can't see and when the wind blows through it, it makes no sound."

The predominant vision of death in Hinduism and Buddhism stands out in bold contrast to this version of the modern view. Hindus and Buddhists see death as anything but "the endless time of never coming back" or "the absence of presence." It is our aim in this paper to investigate a few of the ideas about death and its aftermath which inform these two Eastern traditions and to highlight a few of those notions which we believe might serve some useful purpose for modern man in his search for the recovery of a sense that death is an integral and meaningful part of human life.

## I. DEATH AND REBIRTH IN HINDUISM

*A. Conquest of Death through Sacrificial Offerings in the Vedas.* The earliest phase of Indian religion is recorded in a group of sacred texts known as the *Vedas* (or simply *Veda*), a term that means "sacred knowledge." In those scriptures, the universe is pictured as being a vast, generous and unified cosmos, symbolized by the invocation of the original divine pair, Father Sky and Mother Earth, existing in a perpetual state of embrace. The orderliness and regularity with which the cosmos functioned is epitomized in the concept of Universal Law *(Ṛta)* which exercises unyielding sovereignty over both the cosmos-at-large and human society.

The religion of the Vedic peoples was organized around the fire-cult. The official practices constituting this religious tradition involved the presentation of sacrificial oblations upon the fire altar, which itself symbolized the entire universe in microform dimensions. Hymns of praise and prayers of petition were addressed to various deities believed to embody or to be closely related to the forces of nature (viz., the sun, moon, winds, rains, etc.). The sacrifice seems to have been a kind of contractual agreement between men and gods, whereby, in return for the bestowal of generous amounts of praise and food-offerings, the gods could be expected to maintain the cosmos and provide mankind with all the goods required to support a decent life.

Vedic religion shows itself to be practical minded in its general orientation to the world, manifesting through its prayers, hymns and rituals an extremely healthy affirmation of the reality and goodness of this world. There were little or no signs of world-weariness or spiritual melancholia which pervaded the Upanishads at a later time. The gods were invoked for material bounty: abundance of food and offspring, long life, and protection from the attacks of enemies from the outside. A degree of the consciousness of evil and sin in the world is expressed in the notion that either by neglecting the performance of required sacrifices or the transgression of moral-social law, a person acted unrighteously *(anarta)* namely, contrary to the demands of Universal Law *(Ṛta)*. The "binder" god, Varuṇa held together the entire universe by means of his nooses *(pasas)* and thereby enforced obedience to the cosmic order. He also commanded the service of numerous spies who witnessed the actions of men, submitted those actions to Varuṇa for his judgment and bound with the nooses those persons who transgressed the law of cosmic and social order. Hence, Varuṇa's primary concern was to promote the maintenance of law and order in the universe but, as yet, showed no concern with the *post-mortem* judgment of human deeds.

There are few references to death in Vedic hymns. When the sages mention the topic, they usually make a plea that death overtake their enemies and spare both them and their families for a long life on earth. When the Vedic peoples spoke of the afterlife it was usually imagined to take place in a realm to which those persons went who had pleased the gods while on earth. In this supernatural realm, far removed from the domain of human life, they expected to enjoy pleasures which were an extension of those on earth, different in quantity and duration but not in kind. In more learned circles, death was equated with annihilation or non-being *(asat)*. Life was lived under the aegis of universal law and those who obeyed its dictates could expect to prosper in the hereafter. To die was to be taken beyond the boundaries of the cosmic law into a realm of nothingness.

There are few signs in the sacred texts that Vedic people experienced any profound apprehension or anxiety over the inevitability of death, beyond the use of hymns of praise and sacrificial offerings to postpone the advent of death as long as possible. Their overriding desire was that death should "travel by way of his own special route separated from the way travelled by the gods" and "keep its distance from the living" (RV X.18).

With regard to the eschatology or beliefs concerning the end of the World Age, the Vedic peoples prayed for mercy at the hands of Yama, the god of the dead, who was believed to be "the first mortal to die and enter that other world." The Vedas contain contradictory statements to the effect that Yama's realm was situated both in the midst of the sky or in the highest heaven where the eternal light (i.e. the Sun) abides and, at the same time, in the subterranean regions of the earth, where the ancestors *(pitrs)* dwell. In the early phase of the literature, "that other realm" is pictured as a dazzling paradise, pervaded by undying celestial light, a realm where Yama with the gods, sits down to drink from the waters of a magical river beside a celestial fig tree. Elsewhere in the Rig-Veda and in the later texts, Yama's world is presented in more sombre and even grotesque terms, as a domain of "lowest darkness" and "blind darkness" guarded by two vicious dogs, each possessing four eyes, who test the fitness of all who come that way. One hymn pictures a kind of Hell, as "the house below," inhabited by female goblins and sorceresses, which stands in contrast to the heavenly realm of the gods.

On only one occasion do the scriptures speak of the idea that the soul of the deceased is weighed in the balances and rewarded or punished according as his deeds are good or evil. "In that world, they lay (good and bad deeds) on a balance. Whichever—whether good or bad—draws (down), the consequences are in accordance therewith. But he who knows, he already ascends the balance in this world, (and) renders unnecessary a weighing in that world—his good works prevail, not his bad works." The later ritual texts also make mention of the belief that after death, all persons, both good and bad, are born again in the next world and are recompensed according to their deeds. While the form and agency of *post-mortem* retribution is obscure in the Vedic literature, it is clear that some form of rewards and punishments were meted out to the deceased and that the quality of the life after death was determined by the degree of faithfulness on the part of a person in performing religious rites and moral behavior.

We must note in passing the appearance of an important idea in the later Vedic texts, which was given added significance by the appearance much later in the Upanishads of the notion of the transmigration of the soul; namely, the belief in a second death (*punarmṛtyu*) which is the painful fate of those who, during their lifetime neglected to perform the necessary sacrifices. Whether because of the migration of the Vedic peoples into alien and unknown territories, the ravages of warfare with their enemies, or the recurrence of natural disasters which threatened to destroy their confidence in the good intentions of the gods, it does appear that a profound awareness of the brevity and fragility of life and the certainty of death had begun, by this time, to place in doubt the permanence of *post-mortem* well-being and to raise the specter of having to experience the grim process of dying again and again. The importance of the idea of "re-death" in these early texts lies in the possibility that it may represent an early preview of the doctrine of transmigration (*samsāra*) which involved an endless recurrence of births and deaths for those souls who were trapped by ignorance (*avidyā*).

In general terms, then, the Vedic peoples could be said to have manifested in their sacred literature and religious rituals a vigorous realistic and affirmative view of the world, a quite pragmatic attitude toward the gods with a view toward maintaining a decent and relatively comfortable life in this world, combined with a *willing* acceptance of or, at least, a stoic resignation to, the fate of death. The life of each person was a single occurrence, never to be repeated. Whatever part of the person survived after death was escorted to the land of the dead where it received the fruits of bliss or suffering according to its merits based on both ritual and moral accomplishments or failures. The other world was initially conceived to be both heaven and hell but later was divided to make provision for rewarding the righteous and punishing sinners. Yama, the god of the dead, sent emissaries to call those who were about to die to join him in his celestial kingdom where he might provide them with eternal welfare.

**B. Transcendence of Death through Esoteric Knowledge in the Upanishads.** Toward the latter phases of the Vedic period (ca. 7th–6th centuries B.C.) a series of dramatic innovations occurred which, in time, completely altered the character of Indian religion. Because of an increasing disenchantment with the existing religious establishment, with the centrality of the Brahmanical sacrifice and with the overriding authority of the Brahman priests, there appeared new "schools of thought," the primary concern of which was to discover a principle of life and thought which would serve as a more adequate explanation of the nature of man and the world than the ideology surrounding the sacrifice. The single, most creative and influential discovery to emerge from this series of movements (epitomized by the Upanishads) was the notion that, concealed beneath the constantly changing forms of existence which characterize both human beings and the whole universe, there exists an eternal, changeless something which not only supports but *constitutes* the nature of every living thing.

One of the more provocative attempts to define the nature of this unchanging and indivisible essence of man is found in the Chāndogya Upanishad VIII. 7–12, wherein Prajāpati (the High God in late Vedic literature) instructs Indra (representing the gods) and Virocana (representing the demons) on the nature of the true self. In order to test the knowledge of his two students, Prajāpati identifies the true self as the bodily self (i.e. the mind-body organism that forms the basis of human existence). Indra perceives the hidden error in this teaching by discerning the fact that the self which is subject to both the pleasures and the pains of the body, and the self that perishes with the body, cannot be the real self. Prajāpati next informs Indra that "he who goes about happy in a dream" is the immortal self. But Indra again realizes that this teaching is inadequate. The real self has been discovered by the sages of old to be "free from evil, old age, death, grief, hunger and thirst," whereas this 'dream-life' self shares in every way the sufferings and deprivations of the bodily-self. Indra is then told that perhaps the self is the state of man when "asleep, composed, serene, dreamless." But, he reasons, in that state there is no degree of self-consciousness, no awareness that "I am he" and that person has "gone to annihilation." This "dreaming self" cannot be the real self.

Sensing that Indra is prepared to receive the real truth concerning the nature of the self, Prajāpati informs him: the body is mortal, bound by death and subject to alternation of pleasure and pain, hence, incapable of experiencing true and lasting joy. The body is merely a support for the deathless self. Rising up from his body, he reaches the world of highest light to appear in his own (essential) form as "the Supreme Person." In this realm, "he moves about, laughing, playing, sporting with maidens, chariots, or relations," freed from any recollection of the body, "as an animal is hitched to a wagon, so life is attached to this body." (Chāndogya 8. 12.4–5) In this way, a person finds the Self, understands it truly and, thereby, obtains "all worlds and all desires." In a word, he gains immortality which is understood to be freedom from the chain of rebirth.

The message of this portion of the Upanishads is crucial to an understanding of the Hindu conception of death and the means at man's disposal to deal intelligently with it. Human and animal life, due to the organic connection with the body and with the physical environment, are victimized by all the vicissitudes, fortunes, and misfortunes which are the fate of the body. Because this self is strapped to the body, it undergoes all the changes and transitions from pleasure to pain and back to pleasure, *ad infinitum* without relief or release to which the body is subject. For this self, intoxicated and confused by the dizzying revolutions of the world of the mind and senses, death is no escape. Death can be nothing more than a "way-station" between successive terms of life. A person can expect to escape the sentence of death (lit.: 'redeath') only by discovering and identifying himself with that deep down essential self which is free from evil, death and all the rest, that Absolute One which is both existence and nonexistence, both birth and death. He who discovers the one, changeless, immortal, unnameable *Brahman* ( = cosmic-self) to be identical with the changeless and immortal *ātman* ( = human-self) will be liberated from the sentence of the "Eternal Return," and, on the soul's departure from the world of temporality, birth and death, it will "abide in the world of the *Brahman*."

The coming of death is presented in a most graphic manner in another Upanishad (Bṛhad-āraṇyaka IV. 4 ff.). The approach of death is heralded by a weakening of the body, mind, and senses. As a person approaches death, his senses cease to operate properly. They withdraw from contact with the external world and by gathering around the central core of the self ( = intelligence or consciousness) the person becomes divested of sense-perception little by little. With all the "particles of light" ( = sense organs) concentrated in the heart, the self departs through one of the apertures of the body accompanied by the life-breaths. The person has now become "pure intelligence" due to the concentration of all bodily and mental functions in the seat of consciousness ( = mind). The intelligence now departs into the realm of "absolute space" or "the heavens of the gods," leaving the body behind as a heap of lifeless matter. From there, the self proceeds to enter into a new term of life. The sage concludes this homily on the departure of the soul at death, with these words: "His knowledge, his deeds and his past experience lay hold of him [for the transposition to a new form of existence]."

Then, there follows immediately the presentation of two doctrines which, in time, become the most central ideas in Hindu thought, i.e. the doctrine of rebirth as a consequence of past actions.

Even as a caterpillar, on reaching the tip of a blade of grass, in taking the next step, draws itself up toward itself, so does this self, having cast off this body and having dissolved its ignorance, in taking the next step, draws itself together [for making the transition].

As a goldsmith, taking a piece of gold, transforms it into another newer and more beautiful form, even so this self, casting off this body and dissolving its ignorance, makes for itself another newer and more beautiful form like that of the ancestors or of the heavenly musicians, of the gods of Prajāpati, of Brahmā or of other creatures. (Bṛhadāraṇyaka IV. 4.3–4)

This self, the teacher declares, is the *Brahman*. It constitutes everything that exists but the precise form that it assumes at any given moment and within a particular context depends upon the quality of one's past deeds. "According as one acts, according as he behaves, so does he become. The doer of good becomes good, the doer of evil becomes evil. One becomes virtuous by means of virtuous action, evil by evil action." (Bṛhadāraṇyaka IV. 4.5) There exists a causal relation not only between one's deeds within a given life-term and the results of those deeds realized during the same time-period but also the results accrued in the next lifetime and, perhaps, the one following, until the effects of those deeds have been fully exhausted.

Man, according to this philosophy, consists of desires. As he desires, so does he will; as he wills, so does he act; and as he acts, so does he attain. With the death of the body all the faculties, memories of past experiences and all the fruits of past actions resort to the "subtle body," which undergirds and pervades the "gross" physical body in the form of an ethereal substance. It is this "subtle body" or "subtle mind" (because mind is the central constituent of the subtle body) which serves as the vehicle for transporting the results of the individual's deeds *(karma)* from one life-term into the next. The subtle body survives only as long as the flames of desire are fed by continued search for sensual satisfaction within the physical world. When all desires have been dissolved (especially the desire to perpetuate ego-consciousness which is itself the father of all other desires), then the true inner self *(ātman)* is released from the bonds of rebirth and redeath. That one goes to *Brahman* by becoming *Brahman*, and, thereby, becomes immortal. The self which has freed itself from its body for the last time is likened to a snake which sloughs its skin and leaves it in a lifeless heap on an anthill.

To summarize the teachings of the Upanishads concerning death and rebirth, the soul or spiritual essence *(ātman)* of the individual is eternal. As such, it is unaffected by the various alterations in the state of existence which the phenomenal self or ego *(jīva)* undergoes within each term of life. The mind-body organism which constitutes the person undergoes rebirth as the result of its subjection to the self-deluding belief that it exists as a distinct and independent entity, apart from any kind of relationship to Universal Self. This transmigrating self inherits the fruits of the deeds of previous life cycles and survives the death of the body to experience rebirth in an altered form. The self who has realized its essential identity with the Universal Self enters into a state of spiritual and physical liberation *(moksha)*. On entering the state of liberation, that person is freed from bondage to time, action, rebirth, and redeath. The human actions, both good and bad, cease to have any effect upon his spiritual nature, which now exists in a state that is "in but not of" the world of time and flesh, wholly transcendent to both good and evil. "When all desires that indwell the human heart are cast away, then the mortal becomes immortal and (even) here (in this world) he attains Brahman-hood."

*C. The Realization of Life through Death in the Bhagavad Gītā.* The Bhagavad Gītā, which has come to symbolize the spirit of Hinduism more than any other single Indian religious text, brings together the Path of Works *(karma-mārga)* of the Vedas and the Path of Knowledge *(jñāna-mārga)* of the Upanishads and integrates them to form a single, all-embracing path to salvation. The new doctrine which it introduces for the first time into the Indian religious tradition is the Path of Devotion *(bhakti-mārga)*. In service to the tradition of the Vedas, the Gītā affirms the belief that not only is human action unavoidable (which the followers of the Path of Knowledge tended to deny) but if performed properly, human actions can be expected to produce salutary results. In keeping with the demands of the Path of Knowledge, on the other side, the Gītā asserts that it is not a particular type of human action *per se* that determines the outcome of a course of action, whether for good or ill. Rather, it is the frame of mind and heart (i.e. the moral and spiritual motives) which is crucial. In contrast to the Upanishads, the Gītā contains no idea of the soul achieving liberation from death by going beyond God or gods into the transcendental realm of the Eternal Absolute beyond all distinctions. Rather, it claims that death is conquered and immortality is achieved by identifying oneself with the personal, all-knowing, all-loving God,

Vishnu (in the form of Krishna) in the spirit of faith and in strict obedience to his will.

The idea that the true self (as distinct from the "empirical" self) is eternal and free from the effects of change, is reiterated by Lord Krishna in the Gītā. But, in contradistinction to the teachings of the Upanishads, the Gītā identifies the human self and the "self" (i.e. the essential nature) of the entire universe, with Lord Krishna. Krishna provides instruction on the nature of the self to his student, Arjuna, who is struck with terror by the task of slaying his kinsmen on the field of battle, by declaring that both he who thinks he kills and he who thinks he can be killed, are in error. The undying self cannot be slain by a weapon of warfare: "Never is it born nor does it die; never did it come to be nor will it ever come not to be: Unborn, eternal, everlasting is this primordial [self]. It is not slain when the body is slain." He commands Arjuna to undertake the execution of his duty faithfully, without faltering in the face of death. For, it is not by slaying others, even though they be one's kinsmen, that one is condemned to suffer the pains of hell. Rather, it is by disregarding his duty to God, to his fellowmen and to the World Order *(dharma)*. Man will be redeemed from the condemnation to rebirth by renouncing the fruits of his actions, and, in a spirit of indifference to success and failure, by relying unquestioningly upon the grace of the Lord to eradicate the effects of his deeds *(karma)*. For it is God who is both the initiator of all human actions and the recipient of the fruits of those same deeds. It is He who has the power to cancel out the effects of all human actions and thereby to liberate the eternal and undying soul of man from bondage to rebirth and redeath.

Krishna's argument in brief is that, although the body perishes and can be renovated, the soul *(ātman)* cannot be injured and does not die. Assuming that the Self really did die (which is not the case), that event would be unavoidable because of the fact that all things which come to be in the beginning, pass away in the end. The duty of the warrior, therefore, is to fight and conquer and himself perish on the battlefield. He does not come under the sway of death and rebirth, provided he considers pleasure and pain, gain and loss, victory and defeat to be alike. That person who is unattached psychologically, morally, and spiritually to either birth or death, will incur no sin. The truth of existence which everyone must come to understand if they are to be truly freed from the bonds of ignorance and death is this: "Just as in this body the embodied [self] must pass through childhood, youth, and old age, so too [at death] will it assume another body: about this the wise man is not perplexed." The wise man is one who maintains a state of perfect equilibrium *(samatā)*, in both pleasure and pain, passing through every condition in life, undaunted. Such a person is "fit for immortality." Nor, for that matter, does the wise man mourn the death of others. He lives in the knowledge that "destruction of this imperishable one *(ātman)*, no one can cause." Even where Death does visit itself upon one of the creatures of the world, it does so in obedience to Universal Law and, therefore, is not deserving of human grief. "For certain is the death of all that is born, certain is the birth of all that dies; therefore, with regard to what is inevitable, you have no reason to grieve."

The Gītā propounds the same belief that is central to the teachings of the *Tibetan Book of the Dead* at a much later time. Namely, the frame of mind in which one puts himself just prior to and at the moment of death, will determine the state of being (or non-being) into which he enters after death. "Whatever state (of being) one calls to mind at the end upon leaving aside his body, to that very state he attains, always being made in that state." The dying person is instructed to close all the "doors of the senses," fix the consciousness with the heart-center and stabilize the breath in the head, established in yogic meditation. When he departs this life, with all powers of consciousness and action completely concentrated and the mind fixed upon God (Krishna) alone, "he will travel the highest path" to the highest abode of God beyond the heaven of the gods, from which state "there is no returning." This then, is the "easy way" to salvation, the way of selfless devotion to God and a willing obedience to his will, which is bestowed upon the great majority of persons who find the paths of saintly action or perfection knowledge beyond their grasp. This liberation, which the great priests and sages of the past had claimed for a small elite capable of great spiritual achievements, is now promised to those masses of people who are able to free themselves from attachment to the vicissitudes of pleasure and pain by thinking "upon the Eternal unceasingly," and "thinking of nothing else at all."

**D. The Inevitability of Death in Hindu Mythology.** On a number of occasions in the Hindu epic, the *Mahābhārata*, a sage or a story-teller attempts to assuage the grief of someone who has just lost a comrade or a relative by telling them a story concerning the origin of death. The aim of such stories is to awaken the listener to the fact that death is the fate to which all living creatures come at the appointed time, and the unavoidable gate to another realm or state of being through which all creatures must pass. Therefore, for these reasons, all mourning over the death of an acquaintance or a loved one is wasted.

According to one such story, Brahmā created so many beings that the earth began to fill up to the point that "there was no room to breathe." Since Death had not yet entered the world, multitudinous creatures were being born but none were dying. As a result of the absence of Death, Mother Earth began to feel so overburdened by the weight of this excessive number of creatures that she pled with Brahmā to lighten her load by "removing" a reasonable number of his progeny. He repressed a portion of his creative energy in order to provide for both creation and destruction. Because of an intensification of energy within his being resulting from the repression of energies, a dark maiden dressed in scarlet robes, with eyes blazing red, sprang from his pores. He named her Death and commanded her to "remove" all beings (both wise and foolish) at their appointed time. The maiden Death refused to "remove" the creatures out of a love for them and from a concern that those relatives who remained behind would condemn her actions as unrighteous. She then retired from the world in order to undertake a life of ascetic contemplation.

After urging and cajoling her for years to perform her assigned duty, Brahmā finally transformed Death's tears of grief into diseases and commanded her to use these as instruments for removing the beings. She was also instructed to visit the creatures with the vices of Desire and Wrath before inflicting them with the death-bringing diseases. In this way, the fate of death which comes to every being would be justified on the basis of their unrighteousness. The story-teller concludes with the moral: "Knowing this fact [that death comes to everyone and is a just retribution for sinful deeds], a person should not grieve. For even as the five senses disappear when the person is in deep sleep, later to return to life once the person awakens, even so, in like manner, the creatures with the death of their bodies go from this world into another world and return from there again in due time."

This provocative story of the origin of Death yields an abundance of insights into the Hindu view of Death and the estimation of the necessity and value of death as a functional part of the natural process which was widely accepted at the time of the composition of the Mahābhārata. (ca. 300 B.C.–300 A.D.) We will pause only long enough to cite a few of these points before passing on to a consideration of Buddhist doctrines concerning death.

(1) While the Creator of the world cannot bring himself to destroy his own creation, he would do so quite inadvertently, were he to fail to

find a means of removing a certain number of the products of his creativity in order to make room for those who come later. (This story reflects an awareness on the part of the ancient Indian sages that the absence of a degree of restraint in the production of creatures both animal and human, would gradually result in a "population explosion" which, in turn, would paradoxically lead to the death of the very same creatures which the Creator God had produced.) Without the establishment of an operative balance between the workings of the powers of birth and death, the world of living beings would soon choke to death on the excessive creativity of the creator himself.

(2) Hence, although rebirth *(samsāra)* is considered by Hindus to be an unfortunate destiny which every person should strive to escape at the earliest possible opportunity, these same sages recognized the equally paradoxical fact that without providing the creatures with a means to be reborn, there would be no occasion to strive for the realization of spiritual liberation *(moksha)*. In other words, the very possibility of achieving liberation from ignorance and death rests upon the precondition that mankind be granted a succession of opportunities to make a gradual advance in the direction of that goal. Hence, death is to be viewed as both a necessity and a blessing.

(3) Even though Hindus from every walk of life traditionally have believed that yogic meditation and a life of ascetic withdrawal is the most effective and efficient path to spiritual liberation, the equally important claim is made in this story that, were everyone or even a majority of persons to follow the path of asceticism, the human species would soon become extinct, the laws of society (caste laws, religious rituals, etc.) would languish in the state of neglect and finally, the entire world would slip back into the state of chaos. Therefore, the pursuance of salvation by means of the path of asceticism and self-denial by a special few must be counterbalanced by a provision for the continued procreation and removal of the creatures in the world-at-large.

(4) Death comes to the creatures who inhabit the finite world not because of the inviolable law of fate, or by the ruthless judgment of an angry god but as the result of the moral and spiritual quality of each person's own deeds. It is an individual's *karma* that is the fundamental cause of birth and death. And, for the time being, until all creatures have liberated themselves from the law of rebirth, a provision must be made both for the coming-to-be and the passing-away of things, for the sake of the well-being of the world.

## II. DEATH, REBIRTH AND LIBERATION IN BUDDHIST DOCTRINE

There is general agreement between Hinduism and Buddhism that no human life can be filled with a sense of meaning and efficacious action unless it is lived in full acceptance of the fact of death. He who tries to ignore death by deluding himself into believing that he, his relatives, and his possessions will endure forever, robs himself of the purposeful life which can come only to him who unflinchingly accepts death as an integral part of life. On the other hand, that person who faces death calmly, courageously, and confidently—desiring neither to flee it nor to rush into its grasp—will come to recognize death not as an enemy or a robber but as an ever-present companion and ultimately, as a friend. To meet death, not only as an event at the end of life but as an ever-present ingredient in the life-process itself, is the final goal to be sought in both Hinduism and Buddhism.

Buddhist doctrine defines death as a cutting off of the life-force or a total nonfunctioning of the physical body and the mind. Not that the life-force is totally destroyed with the death of the body; it is merely displaced and transformed to continue functioning in another form. Every birth is, in fact, a rebirth. Many Buddhists believe that rebirth occurs immediately after death. Others believe that forty-nine days separate death and rebirth in an "intermediary state" *(Bardo)*, graphically described in the *Tibetan Book of the Dead*, about which we will speak in greater detail presently.

Birth and death, when viewed at the cosmic level of perception, describes the outer limits of the life of both the individual person and of the cosmos. Strictly speaking, neither human beings nor the universe itself experiences either an absolute beginning or an absolute end. When this same drama of birth and death is viewed as the microlevel in terms of seconds and fractions of seconds rather than years or aeons, birth and death are discovered to occur almost simultaneously in each instant of time. The human person is nothing more than a conglomeration of "aggregates" (i.e. body, sensations, perceptions, mental formations, and consciousness) which, taken together form the mind-body organism engaged in the process of coming-to-being and passing-away in every moment.

But, according to Buddhist teachings, there is no single permanent, unchanging entity or substance constituting the Self or Soul which endures in a uniform state from moment to moment and from lifetime to lifetime. That phenomenon which we customarily call "the self" in speaking of "I myself" or "you yourself" is nothing more than a continuity of a series of psycho-physiological occasions (described by the American psychologist, William James, as "the stream of consciousness") which undergoes an unbroken series of alterations in every moment. As one teacher states it: "When the Aggregates arise, decay and die, O monk, every moment you are born, decay and die." Thus, in every instant we are born; in every instant we die. Birth and death are two almost indistinguishable and imperceptible strands of a single rope of existence.

The human self, therefore, is composed of a stream of consciousness, changing momentarily and filled with impressions and tendencies created by good and evil actions *(karma)* which at death is transposed to a new mode of being, while the imagined "self" who thinks in terms of "I" and "mine" does not survive from one moment to the next and hence, does not transmigrate.

The Buddhists, like the Hindus, believe that there are differences in the quality of deaths, just as there are differences in the quality of births and existences. The differences in deaths depends upon the difference between disciplined and undisciplined living, between pure and impure mind or between "carefulness" and "carelessness." "Carefulness is the path of the deathless; carelessness is the path to death . . . The constantly meditative, the ever earnestly striving ones, realize the bond-free, supreme Nirvana" *(Dhammapada* 21–23).

The "soul" or "the fruits of the karma" of a deceased person who is still trapped by the bonds of "desire," according to popular Buddhist belief, will go immediately after death to Yama's judgment chamber where, after a waiting period of seven days, he is required to cross a treacherous river with three current speeds simultaneously (representing three karmic destinies of hell: human beings, animals and hungry ghosts). Those who cross the river successfully are ushered into a Paradise or a Happy Land, ruled by Amitābha ("Boundless Light") who will provide a rebirth in his Paradise for those who have true faith in him and praise his holy name.

All of this is by way of saying that for Gautama, the Buddha, the way to an effective life within this world and to a final release from the curse of rebirth beyond this world leads through a calm and confident recognition of the universal truth that, "all composite things must pass away." The truly Awakened One is that person who recognizes that, indeed, the whole universe is passing away, that nothing remains as it is for more than an instant and that, for this reason, nothing which abides within this realm of death is deserving of a person's absolute trust. This is the Truth which Gautama foresaw during his legendary "pleasure excursion" when he witnessed the four signs of suffering: poverty, sickness, old age, and death. On that occasion, he experienced a total loss of confidence in the reality and value of existence in the finite world because of his discovery that everything is "subject to change and decay" and death "is the end which has been fixed for all." He sighed to his charioteer: ". . . and yet the world forgets its fear and takes no heed. The hearts of men are surely hardened to fears, for they feel quite at ease even while travelling along the road to the next life . . ."

The message of the Buddha to all suffering humanity is this: everything inevitably comes to extinction even though it may last for a millennium. Everything must be parted from what it desires in the end. Recognize that all living things (mineral, vegetable, animal, human, and divine) are subject to the law of death. Therefore, recognize the true nature of the living world and do not be anxious about your life or your death. "When the light of true knowledge has dispelled the darkness of ignorance, when all existence has been seen as without substance, peace ensues when life draws to an end, which seems to cure a long illness at last. Everything, whether stationary or movable is bound to perish in the end. Be ye therefore mindful and vigilant." (*Buddhacārita* XXVI 88 ff.)

Men are instructed by the Buddha not to make any plans in this world without reckoning with death. For death comes according to the dictates of time, unannounced and unanticipated by most persons. How can one know beforehand when death will strike: whether today or tomorrow, one year or five years hence or within the next moment? How can one anticipate the form that death will take: a mortal wound from a knife or a gun, an automobile accident, a lingering illness or a sudden heart-attack? Death strikes without notice; the young and the old, the well and the sickly, the high and the low, the wealthy and the poor. It is no respecter of persons. There is no lasting peace as long as the person is still in the body. Therefore, one should not place any trust in a life which is sustained by so uncertain a thing as breathing in and out.

This doctrine of the inevitability of death for all living creatures is movingly expressed in one of the most popular of all Buddhist stories, the "Parable of the Mustard Seed." According to this story, a woman is discovered grieving uncontrollably over the death of her beloved son whose corpse she carries in her arms. She does not seem to be aware that death is a terminal event—for this lifetime, at least. In hopes of

finding an antidote to her child's "malady" which would restore him
to consciousness, she approaches the Buddha who is renowned for his
miraculous powers to heal. The Buddha does provide her with an
antidote, but not the sort that she has sought. He instructs her to go
from house to house throughout the city in search of a few grains of
mustard seed. The mustard seeds, he says, will provide the proper
antidote to the child's disease (i.e. death). But, she must accept the
mustard seed only from a household in which no one has ever
died—not a father or a mother, not a brother or a sister, not a servant
or an animal. After searching from house to house, she discovers that
not a single household can be found which has never experienced the
death of one of its members. In time she comes to see the truth which is
the panacea to death and sorrow: that death is the inescapable destiny
of all creatures and that, given its inevitability, she has no cause to
grieve. Relieved from the pangs of both false-hope and needless grief,
she goes immediately with peace of mind, to the burning-ground and
there submits her son to the fires of cremation.

The ideal which every being caught in the net of rebirth should
strive to realize is the "cutting of the root of desires" by recognizing
the transitory, unpredictable, and insubstantial nature of the existence
of everything in the finite world. This ideal of "desirelessness" is
epitomized in Theravāda Buddhism by the Arhat ("Worthy One")
and in Mahāyāna Buddhism by the Bodhisattva ("He Whose Essence
is Wisdom"). The "Awakened One" has no desires whatsoever, either
to be attached to what gives him pleasure or to be separated from
what gives him pain. Having no likes or dislikes, he is not subject to
the pincers of hope and anxiety, ambition and frustration. He "does
not shake down the unripe fruit . . . (but) waits for it to mature," such
that he is able to say:

> It is not death, it is not life I cherish.
> I bide my time, a servant waiting for his wages.
> It is not death, it is not life I cherish.
> I bide my time in mindfulness and wisdom steeped.

Buddhist teachers through the ages have claimed that the most
effective means of arriving at this state of desirelessness is to cultivate
mental and physical discipline through meditation. One of the most
widely used forms of meditation among Buddhist monks is "the
recollection of death." The monk is instructed to seat himself in the
graveyard or the crematorium and contemplate upon the ashes of the

bodies that have been disposed of and upon the corpses which still lie about the area in various states of decay. By contemplating upon these foul substances, the meditator quickly becomes profoundly aware of the brevity, uncertainty, and impermanence of life and the inevitability of death. The monk is often instructed to consider his own body, though still full of life and vigor, to be a (potential) corpse. When the monk realizes within the deepest part of his being that his own life and that of the entire universe is constituted and supported by a compound of birth and death in each and every moment, and when he comes to know that in the end everything returns to ashes, he will obtain a perfect freedom *(vimukti)* from the illusion that he and the objects of his pleasure are enduring entities. From this insight emerges a cessation of desire to wield the world according to one's own volition. And, with the passing of this habit of living a life of willfulness (and its offspring anxiety and fear) will come automatically a peace of mind and tranquility which will abide unaltered in all conditions of life and all states of mind.

Finally, the various Buddhist teachings concerning death and the most efficacious way of "living toward death" are presented in a most imaginative manner in the book which is currently purchased by more people in the western world than any other work, with the possible exception of the Bible, namely, *The Tibetan Book of the Dead.* As the title indicates, this text is to be used in teaching the living "how to die well." The text is used most particularly in helping those who are elderly, feeble, or sick to prepare in themselves a state of mind that will be most conducive to a "good rebirth" or to a liberation from rebirth altogether.

The teacher instructs his student to remain watchful and alert in the face of death, to resist all forms of distraction and confusion, to be lucid and calm. He further charges the student to realize that his "mental energies" or "life-forces" are about to disengage from the body. In order that he might enter the "intermediate state" well-prepared, he should rouse his energy and focus his consciousness upon the event of his passing. The instructor then urges the student to prepare himself for the coming of death in the form of "the brilliant light of Ultimate Reality" or "the luminous splendor of the colorless light of Emptiness." He must immerse himself in the rays of that supernatural light, abandoning all belief in a separate self and recognize that salvation comes from the realization that that "boundless light of this true Reality is your own true self".

For those whose minds are diverted or confused at this moment of passage into the other world, there emerges a "subtle body" or a "mental body" which is "impregnated with the after-effects of your past deeds and desires." These supernatural bodies are but the light-rays cast off from the grace of the Buddhas who have come to receive the soul of the deceased into a Buddha-realm or Paradise (Happy Land). If this second opportunity for salvation is missed, the soul is then attacked by angry deities and demonic creatures (some of them in the form of fearsome animals) who attempt to divert the soul from salvation by convincing it that these creatures are objectively real, when in fact they are nothing more than "imaginary reflections of the contents of the mind in the mirror of the Void."

Two destinies are open to the soul at this point: (1) it can achieve total and eternal cessation of rebirth together with the peace of Nirvāṇa by realizing that all things (including these heavens and hells, gods and demons, births and deaths, etc.) are illusory, insubstantial and transitory projections of his own limited and perverted mind; or (2) it is doomed once again, to re-enter the wheel of becoming to be reborn as an animal, a man or a god, because of its twofold failure to grasp the meaning of these teachings and to free itself from the desire to perpetuate itself as an individual self.

The essence of the Buddhist teaching about death is expressed beautifully in a sermon by the famous Zen master of the thirteenth century, Dōgen:

To find release you must begin to regard life and death as identical to Nirvāna, neither loathing the former nor coveting the latter. It is fallacious to think that you simply move from birth to death. Birth, from the Buddhist point of view, is a temporary point between the preceding and succeeding; hence, it can be called 'birthlessness.' The same holds for death and deathlessness. In life there is nothing more than life, in death nothing more than death: we are being born and dying at every moment.

## III. THE CONQUEST OF DEATH

The teachings of Hinduism and Buddhism seem to sound a single but antiphonal theme. The stories and instructional discourses which constitute the sacred literature of both traditions, assert, on the one hand, that death is the unavoidable fate of every living creature and that its iron rule cannot be broken by any means—whether by good works, pious thoughts, or spiritual discipline. On the other hand, it is claimed that, even though all creatures are destined to pass away, there is a means of escaping death in the form of rebirth. The primary cause of rebirth—and all of its attendant sufferings and misfortunes— is egotism. The only truly effective escape from this round of birth and death is the dissolution of all desires. Properly understood, the path to final liberation leads at last to the dissipation of that last desire, with the result that one enters a state of existence which can only be described as "desireless."

For the most part, the conquest of death is believed to be a long and arduous task, involving the cultivation of a disciplined mind and body throughout many terms of existence. The practice of virtue does bring its reward in the form of religious merit. With a sufficient amount of merit in hand, one can expect to enjoy material and spiritual prosperity in heaven after death. But, this is not the ultimate goal to be reached according to Hindu and Buddhist teachings. Beyond this world of living beings, beyond the atmosphere populated by demigods and spirits, even beyond the highest heavens inhabited by higher gods and the High God himself, there exists a supernal realm of eternal, unalloyed Bliss. However demanding the task of realizing that distant goal may be, a word of encouragement is offered in the doctrine of transmigration in Hinduism and rebirth in Buddhism. Krishna sums up the idea succinctly in the *Bhagavad Gītā*: "And even if you think it [the embodied self] is continually [re-] born and constantly [re-] dies, even so you grieve for it in vain. For certain is the death of all that is born, certain is birth of all that dies; so in a matter that no one can prevent, you have no cause to grieve" (II. 27).

Disregarding for the moment the single most important point of contention which distinguishes the Hindus and the Buddhists (i.e. whether or not there is a real self which survives from one lifetime to the next), both traditions agree in general, on the most effective method of conquering death: accept death as the chief fact of life and as the main signal that all the things you hope for will be utterly destroyed in due course and that once you come to be able to neither long for nor fear death, you are beginning to transcend both life and death and coming into unity with the Changeless Absolute. Human nature is composed of desires. As a man desires, so he wills. As he wills so he acts. As he acts, so does he become. That person is bound in the chains of death, the fears of his own death, and the grief over the death of others, who tries to ignore death. That person is freed from the fetters of death and all its attendant anxieties, who meets death as a companion to life, in the spirit of rational and tranquil acceptance, without clinging to or fleeing it. This seems to be a most valuable lesson to be learned by those who live in this modern era when the preservation of human life by the postponement or escape from death is pursued at all costs.

## SUGGESTED READINGS

### *I. Hinduism*

BASHAM, A. L. *The Wonder that was India.* New York: Grove Press, 1959.

EMBREE, A. T. *The Hindu Tradition: Readings in Oriental Thought.* New York: Random House, 1966.

HOPKINS, T. J. *The Hindu Religious Tradition.* Belmont, California: Dickenson Publishing Co., 1971.

ZAEHNER, R. C. *Hinduism.* London: Oxford University Press, 1962.

### *II. Buddhism*

CONZE, E. *Buddhism in Essence and Development: Buddhist Scriptures.* Baltimore: Penguin Books, 1959.

DE BARY, T. *The Buddhist Tradition in India, China and Japan.* New York: Random House, 1969.

RAHULA, W. *What the Buddha Taught.* New York: Grove Press, 1959.

ROBINSON, R. H. *The Buddhist Religion. A Historical Introduction.* Belmont, California: Dickenson Publishing Co., 1970.

# 4
# Dying Is Easy, but Living Is Hard

We've been talking about the difficulty of dealing with death in this society, and we've offered some alternative views of death that might help you understand it in a different perspective from that ordinarily taken. But regardless of your perspective, it's not really the dying that's so hard; dying takes no skill and no understanding. It can be done by anyone. What is hard is living—living until you die, whether your death is imminent or a long way off; whether it's you who are dying or one you love. The different views of death and dying we gave you in the preceding chapter hopefully made you think about living as well as dying—how you might borrow from other cultural customs and perspectives to make living until death more meaningful for yourself and those you care for.

In this chapter we will again look at death within our own culture, but from some more death-accepting, life-affirming points of view than we normally encounter. We will look from institutional *and* personal points of view at some of the factors that can contribute to a fuller life for those who are dying as well as a fuller acceptance and understanding of death for those who are left behind in this life. In the first selection, the *Living until Death Program* is described; it is a research study to determine what factors make a difference in the lives of dying patients and to apply these findings to helping dying patients live out their lives more joyfully and peacefully. The second selection explains how the funeral and all the tasks surrounding it can play an important part in the growth toward peace and acceptance of the bereaved. In the third selection, a mother struggles with her grief and grows; we share some of her groping attempts at finding equilibrium after her son's death. Finally, the last selection of the chapter shows the continued growth of a writer and a human being as she approaches death; Dorothy Pitkin's last writings reveal a human being still puzzling over the meaning of life in the perspective of many creative years.

The one thread that seems to weave its way through all these selections, different though they are, is the necessity of truthfulness and straightforwardness. You cannot learn to accept death when you avoid it and deny it. You must face death squarely if you are to deal with it constructively. Whether it is you who are dying, one you love, or one in your professional care, it will be difficult. The end of a life is not something any of us can easily accept. But the fact does not go away if you ignore it, and the real challenge is to fully live the time you have. One of the early responses many people have to death is despair. It is easy, at this point, to give up on living because there doesn't seem to be enough time left. Learning to throw off that feeling of despair and replace it with one of joy at the opportunity to really live, if only for a short time, is hard but extremely rewarding. Learning to reinvest yourself in living when you have lost someone you love is very difficult, but only through doing so can you give some meaning to that person's death. I hope that the following selections will help you understand better how to face and deal with death whenever it becomes a part of your life.

# Living Until Death: A Program of Service and Research for the Terminally Ill

## Raymond G. Carey

*In this selection the author describes a study of terminally ill patients. The aim is to discover what factors predict who will best cope with dying and what can be done by helping professionals to make life more meaningful for dying patients. The results are consistent with information derived from various other sources presented in this book. For example, the findings suggest that dying patients should be allowed as much control as possible over their lives and routines, and life should, as far as possible, be consistent with the life they led before their illness; this applies especially to their relationships with important people in their lives and being allowed to spend as much time as possible in familiar and comfortable surroundings. This finding fits well with the description in the preceding chapter of the ease with which the Alaskan Indians faced death because of their sense of choice and control. Another important point, reconfirmed in many selections, is that patients are generally more comfortable about their fate when they feel their physician has been honest, yet reassuring with them. A primary factor, of concern to physicians and nurses caring for dying patients, is the amount of pain an individual has; it is very difficult to maintain emotional equilibrium when you are in extreme pain. There are other important factors, and this article offers advice to helping professionals on what they can do to help. When you read this selection, try to keep in mind what you've already learned, and see what parallels you can find.*

## THE LIVING UNTIL DEATH PROGRAM

People who are informed they have a limited life expectancy react ın

"Living until Death: A Program of Service and Research for the Terminally Ill," by Raymond G. Carey, Ph.D., Director of Evaluation and Research Services, Lutheran General Hospital, Park Ridge, Illinois, and a diocesan priest in the Archdiocese of Chicago. This essay first appeared as an article in *Hospital Progress* in February 1974. Reprinted by permission of the author.

different ways. Some seem to be able to cope adequately with the psychic pain that may come in the form of anger, depression, fear, or inappropriate guilt. They adjust emotionally to the point that they are able to live the final weeks and months of their lives with inner tranquility. Other patients seem unable to handle this pain. The terminally ill patient, by definition, cannot be helped to regain physical well-being. However, he can be helped to live his life as fearlessly and fully as possible until he dies.

To assist terminal patients in this manner, a more accurate understanding of the factors related to emotional adjustment is needed. For example, what is the importance of (1) the amount of discomfort the patient experiences, (2) religious attitudes and beliefs, (3) previous experience with dying persons, (4) financial security, (5) age, (6) sex, and (7) education? Further, it would help to have a clearer picture of the anxieties of terminal patients and the manner in which these anxieties are related to a person's age, sex, and religious values. The Living Until Death Program was designed to explore these questions.

The Living Until Death Program is a research project incorporated into a program of service. Every patient at Lutheran General Hospital receives a visit from a chaplain who is prepared to offer a varied ministry to both patient and family: counseling, prayer, and sacraments. The Living Until Death Program requires that, in addition to standard pastoral care, the chaplain: (1) offer his service as counselor specifically to deal with the patient's feelings regarding his serious illness; (2) continue the established relationship in the event the patient leaves the hospital; (3) offer the patient the opportunity to help others by sharing his feelings through answering an orally-administered questionnaire or by making an audiotape or videotape when this seems possible and appropriate.

The chaplains who are part of this program are not primarily concerned with helping the patients prepare for death, but rather with helping them live each day as joyfully and peacefully as possible. They also try to help the family of the patient deal with their feelings in such a way as to bring comfort to both patient and relatives.

Little quantitative research has been conducted with patients who are terminally ill to examine emotional adjustment to a limited life expectancy. Almost all previous research has used a case study approach. The present research attempted to identify, through analysis of quantitative data, factors that correlate with emotional adjustment in the terminal patient who knows his condition.

## METHOD AND PROCEDURE

In this research project a terminally ill person is defined as one whose illness is such that: (1) death is probable within a year, if the unwholesome condition persists; and (2) there is no known cure for the patient's condition. Only patients who were aware of the seriousness of their condition were candidates for the program. Patients who were unaware of the potential fatality of the illness, who were *in extremis*, or who were too weak or sedated for counseling were not considered as candidates for the research aspect of the program.

The offer of counseling was made to 84 candidates between December 15, 1972 and July 31, 1973. Table I gives a profile of these patients. Referrals were made by student chaplains, head nurses, and physicians. The Chairman of the Division of Pastoral Care selected chaplains who worked under the direction of the project director in contacting proposed candidates. Eleven chaplains (nine Lutherans and two Catholics) were involved in the program over the period of eight months.

The principal method of research was analysis of quantitative data obtained from patients by hospital chaplains. However, four videotape and four audiotape interviews were made with patients about their main anxieties and sources of strength. These tapes enabled the project director to form an evaluation of emotional adjustment independent from that made by the counseling chaplain. They also helped in interpreting the results of quantitative analysis. However, the tapes were not the main method of research.

## MEASURES AND STATISTICAL ANALYSIS

The main dependent variable in this study was the Emotional Adjustment (EA) Scale. The scale was designed to measure the extent to which a terminal patient was able to cope interiorly and exteriorly with his limited life expectancy. Emotional adjustment includes the concept of inner peace and self-possession, but it is not the same as resignation, acceptance, or despair of recovery.

The EA Scale consisted of six questions which the chaplain rated on the basis of the patient's words and behavior, as well as on information obtained from the staff and the patient's family. The questions measured the presence or absence of anger, guilt, anxiety, depression, and also the ability of the patient to verbalize his feelings with family and friends.

TABLE I
PROFILE OF PATIENTS

Total number—84
Percent given in parentheses

| | | N | % |
|---|---|---|---|
| Offer of counseling | accepted | 74 | (88) |
| | rejected | 10 | (12) |
| Sex | male | 42 | (50) |
| | female | 42 | (50) |
| Marital status | single | 9 | (11) |
| | married | 57 | (68) |
| | widow(er)s | 14 | (17) |
| | separated or divorced | 4 | ( 5) |
| Age | 13–19 | 3 | ( 4) |
| | 20–29 | 4 | ( 5) |
| | 30–39 | 8 | (10) |
| | 40–49 | 13 | (16) |
| | 50–59 | 22 | (26) |
| | 60 and over | 34 | (41) |
| Amount of education | grammer school | 9 | (13) |
| | high school | 31 | (45) |
| | college | 23 | (33) |
| | post-grad work | 6 | ( 9) |
| | no information | 15 | — |
| Type of illness | cancer | 77 | (92) |
| | other diseases | 7 | ( 8) |
| Religious affiliation | Lutheran | 18 | (21) |
| | other Protestant | 23 | (27) |
| | Catholic | 31 | (37) |
| | Jewish | 5 | ( 6) |
| | none | 7 | ( 8) |

The discomfort scale was formed from five items. The chaplains evaluated the patient's amount of pain, disfigurement, dependence on others, difficulty in eating, and difficulty in sleeping.

The relationship between religion and emotional adjustment was examined from the aspect of religious affiliation, religious beliefs, and the quality of religious orientation. Four categories of religious orientation (RO) were considered: intrinsic, extrinsic, indiscriminately pro-religious, and indiscriminately non-religious. Gordon Allport characterized an intrinsically religious person as one who takes seriously the commandment of brotherhood, strives to transcend self-centered needs, tempers his dogma with humility, and seems to live the teachings of his faith. The extrinsically orientated person is characterized by Allport as one who takes a self-centered approach to life, looking after his own personal safety, social standing, and chosen way of life. This person seeks to use religion rather than to live it. It is a utilitarian orientation to religion.

In this study a revised form of the original Allport scale was used to measure religious orientation. The RO measure was scored by summing each patient's total for both the intrinsic and extrinsic subscales. Patients were classified as intrinsic or extrinsic if they scored above the median on one of these scales, but not on the other. They were indiscriminately pro-religious if above the median on both scales, indiscriminately non-religious if below the median on both scales.

Previous experience with dying persons was analyzed from three standpoints: (1) whether or not the patient had ever talked frankly and openly about death with someone else who knew he or she was dying; (2) whether or not he was close to someone who accepted death with inner peace; and (3) whether or not he had been close to someone who was angry or upset to the end of his life.

Ratings of occupational status obtained from the National Opinion Research Center were used as an indirect measure of financial security.

## SUMMARY OF PRINCIPAL FINDINGS

*1. What were the main factors that predicted emotional adjustment to a limited life expectancy?* The most important factors in predicting emotional adjustment were the level of discomfort, previous close contact with a person who was dying, religious orientation, a feeling of great interest and concern on the part of one's nearest of kin and local clergyman, and amount of education.

Level of discomfort was negatively related to emotional adjustment. That is, the more discomfort an individual suffered, the less able he was to maintain a high level of emotional adjustment. Having been close to a person who accepted death with inner peace was a positive factor in emotional adjustment, while having been close to a dying person who was angry and upset was a negative factor. Female patients who had previously discussed death openly and frankly with another dying person had much greater ability to cope with their own terminal illnesses. The most important aspect of the religious variable was the quality of religious orientation, rather than mere religious affiliation or verbal acceptance of religious beliefs. Intrinsically religious persons (those who tried to integrate their beliefs into their life styles) had the greatest emotional adjustment. However, Christians had much higher emotional adjustment than non-Christians. Education was also positively related to emotional adjustment, possibly because both are related to financial security.

*2. What are the main anxieties of terminal patients?* The most frequently expressed concern was the fear of being a burden to others. Two-thirds of the patients expressed great or extreme anxiety regarding this possibility. About 50 percent of patients expressed great concern about being separated from their loved ones, about how loved ones will care for themselves after the patient's death, and about a painful death. Chaplains' reports indicate that the feeling that life no longer has any value or meaning was an underlying concern of many.

*3. What did the audiotapes and videotapes reveal concerning emotional adjustment?* An analysis of audiotape and videotape interviews indicated that the following factors are of importance in emotional adjustment: ability to cope with stressful situations in the past, the feeling of having lived a meaningful and fulfilled life, a warm and supporting relationship with one's spouse, hope of a joyful life after death, the ability to talk frankly about the meaning and consequences of one's illness, an explanation from one's physician that combines tactful candor with assurance of support, and a feeling of concern from one's children and close friends. Anxieties were expressed more often about the process of dying than about what would happen after death. Many patients were concerned with how much pain there would be in the future, how they would be able to cope with this pain, how dependent they would become, and how much of a burden they would become to others.

Making audiotapes and videotapes seemed to have a very positive effect on the morale of patients. In most cases the immediate family asked to have an audiotape copy of their loved one's interview and said they found great comfort in listening to the tape.

## EVALUATION AND SUGGESTIONS FOR PATIENT CARE

*1. What are the main challenges facing a terminal patient?* The patient must first decide whether he is going to accept or reject the reality of dying. Denial involves the attitude, "I *am* going to get better," in spite of all information to the contrary. The *desire* to recover may be present even with acceptance.

Secondly, the patient must find satisfactory meaning in his new life situation, that is, in the pain, helplessness, changing relationships, separations, and losses. In other words, he must find an answer to the gnawing question, "Of what value am I now?" If the patient finds a satisfactory answer to this question, he has acquired emotional adjustment, whether he is in a state of acceptance or denial.

*2. Where does a patient find help in acquiring emotional adjustment?* Each patient is different. He finds help in his own way, in his own resources, and sets his own order of helping agents. There are four sources of help that are cited most frequently: religious faith (God, church, clergy); one's spouse (or other family member); oneself (thinking through the problem, figuring it out intellectually); and the physician who is straightforward and honest, while at the same time considerate of the patient's capacity to handle his diagnosis.

*3. What can the chaplain do to assist terminal patients?* First of all, the chaplain ought to learn where the patient is emotionally and how he sees his situation. He must respect the patient's feelings and thoughts and help him to find and use his own resources, religious or not.

He must show the patient he cares by coming regularly to talk and to listen to him. He must be sensitive in responding to the patient's changing moods.

It is important that the chaplain be willing to share the helping with others: family members, the patient's clergyman, nurses, aides, and social workers. The chaplain's specialty is dealing with ultimate concerns (the meaning of life and death), but other people will fill some needs of the patient better than he.

A special concern of the chaplain will be to help the patient see that there can be meaning and value simply in how one copes with suffering and death. However, the chaplain must not push himself, his own ideas, his own feelings, or his own solutions. The content of his counseling must be guided by the needs and desires of the patient. The patient must sense that his own way and style of dealing with his dying are acceptable to the chaplain, although the chaplain is available to help him look at alternatives, if the patient wishes. The chaplain should be available to share his own faith and resources, such as prayer, Scripture, Communion, if the patient desires them.

Another important point is for the chaplain to cultivate the trust and cooperation of physicians. He should avoid talking about medical questions with patients. He should be at the nursing station when the physician is there and ask the physician how he feels the patient is handling his illness and how the chaplain might help. On the other hand, the chaplain must not hesitate to say what he feels he can do to help. It is advisable to keep the physician informed of the chaplain's activities either by writing on the ecology sheet of the patient's chart or by seeing the physician in person.

*3. How can the family assist the patient to adjust emotionally?* The family can help most by maintaining an emotional and social environment consistent with the patient's past life style, when circumstances permit. Specifically, this means keeping the patient at home where he can eat and sleep as normally as possible, rather than in the hospital or nursing home. Unless the patient is no longer mentally alert, the family should include him as a participant in discussions and decisions about his care and welfare. It is important for the family to do all they can to show their love and concern without doing it in such a way as to make the patient feel guilty because he thinks he is becoming a burden to them.

Family members who cannot face death in their own lives and project this fear on their loved one can be an obstacle to the patient's effort to handle his own psychic pain. This attitude can also make it difficult for a physician to be honest with his patient and for a chaplain to do effective counseling. When the patient is ready to accept the reality of dying, the family must be ready to share his acceptance.

*4. What can physicians do to help the patient adjust emotionally?* There seems to be little doubt that most people want to hear the truth from their physicians. Only one patient in this study expressed anger with her physician for telling her she had a limited life expectancy. However, the manner in which the information is given is critical. It seems best to do it in person, rather than over the phone, and allow time for the patient to express his feelings and ask questions. When possible, it seems advisable for the physician to prepare his patient gradually, for example, by letting the patient know that cancer is a possibility and at the same time outlining proposed treatment in the event that suspicions are verified. Patients want to be reassured that their physician will not give up on them.

Physicians may all too readily agree to a family's request to hide the truth from a patient. Counseling dying patients and their families is time consuming and often unrewarding both financially and emotionally for physicians. If the physician feels that he does not have the time or the training to provide effective counseling for the patient and family, he is well advised to refer them to someone who can meet this need. Referral to oncologists or radiation therapists at times can be used as escapes from facing the need for counseling.

This study indicates that proper administration of pain medication is a major factor in emotional adjustment. The number one predictor of emotional adjustment is a low level of discomfort. Anxiety about how much pain there will be and how well it can be endured ranks high on the list of patient concerns. A patient will have greater peace if he knows that his suffering will be kept at bearable levels.

Finally, physicians should be willing to seek or accept the help of chaplains and other paramedical personnel. The patient has many needs. No one, including physicians, can possibly be expert in meeting every need.

*5. Are local clergy needed in hospitals where there are an adequate number of well-trained chaplains?* Local clergymen complement the ministry of hospital chaplains in assisting terminal patients, particularly in those instances where they have had a good past relationship with the patient. Rapport is already established. Visiting patients and bringing the sacraments to those who value this ministry give a supportive feeling of love and concern. Close contact with a patient's family during the time of terminal illness will be a basis for more effective ministry at the time of the wake and funeral services as well as in the months that follow the patient's death. At these times, the family ordinarily does not have their physician or the hospital chaplain to turn to for strength and comfort. Many patients commented that they appreciated both the ministry of the chaplain and their local clergyman.

*6. How can nurses contribute to the patient's emotional adjustment?* Nurses are at a disadvantage in helping patients to adjust emotionally because they ordinarily do not have the past rapport with the patient that the physicians and local clergy may have nor do they ordinarily have the counseling skills of trained chaplains. However, nurses are often available in moments of crisis and depression when others are not immediately available. This is particularly true at night, or in hospitals where there is inadequate pastoral care. Nurses become more important in a counseling role with patients who do not have close relatives or who have only a shallow or poor relationship with their physicians or local clergy.

Nurses can best help by listening for subtle clues of the patient's feelings and attempting to adapt to his moods, rather than by planning ahead of time what they will say to cheer the patient when they go into his room.

*7. How can social workers and home care personnel help?* The most frequent anxiety expressed by terminal patients in this study was worry about being a burden to others. By providing the patient and his family with information and guidance on available care when the patient leaves the hospital, the social worker and home care personnel are removing a significant obstacle to emotional adjustment. There are also times when it would be possible and appropriate for them to assist in a counseling role.

*8. How can a person prepare himself to cope with terminal illness?* The results of this study indicate that one of the most important things a person can do to prepare himself to cope with terminal illness is to welcome the opportunity to be close to someone who is presently facing terminal illness with inner peace. Talking frankly about death and dying may not only help the patient sort out his own feelings, but also assist the other person to adjust emotionally if he in turn contracts an incurable illness.

If one is the main breadwinner of a family, it seems advisable to plan financially ahead of time, so that dependents will have security in the event of a sudden illness. Removing financial worries eliminates one road block to emotional adjustment.

Integrating religious beliefs into one's life style today may reduce the possibility of guilt and concern about God's anger, increase trust in God's loving care, and sustain a well-founded hope in a life of happiness after death, in the event of terminal illness.

Finally, cultivating deep and loving relationships with family and friends will provide a solid support in the face of death.

*9. Are there critical times when counseling is more likely to be effective?* The time when counseling seems most needed and is most likely to be effective is shortly after the patient has become aware that he has an incurable disease and that death is a possibility in the not too distant future. Very often the full impact of this realization occurs just before or after an operation. It seems advisable to deal with the patient's feelings soon after the physician informs the patient of his condition. It is often easier to prevent anger, bitterness, or depression than it is to help the patient overcome these feelings once they have taken root. If one waits until the patient is very weak or near death before calling the local clergyman or chaplain, his ministry becomes more difficult both with respect to counseling the patient and to opening up a more healthy relationship between the patient and his relatives.

*10. Is it advisable to have a chaplain work exclusively with the terminally ill?* The advantages of having a chaplain work exclusively with terminal patients seem to outweigh disadvantages. A specialized chaplain can engender trust and confidence on the part of physicians and nursing staff more easily. Physicians and nurses are reluctant to call a chaplain to counsel their patients in such a sensitive area, unless they have clear knowledge of his goals, his style of counseling, and an awareness of his competence from past performances. Specializing in terminal illness also makes it easier for the chaplain to gain both knowledge and self-confidence. There are possible disadvantages. For example, there is a danger that patients and relatives may react negatively or give up all hope, if they know they are being visited by a chaplain who only sees "hopeless" cases. There is also the question of whether a chaplain can work only with dying patients and not tend to become depressed himself.

*11. What are the main problems faced in this program?* The main support, as well as the main difficulty, came from physicians. The president of the medical staff, department heads, and some attending physicians were extremely supportive of the program. It was difficult to get the cooperation, support, and trust of many physicians. Some were hostile to any mention of research with the terminally ill. Others were apathetic to the program. It meant one more person to whom they would have to relate in their already overcrowded schedules. Some had incorrect information on the nature of the questionnaire and how it was administered.

Another problem was the difficulty in deciding who were candidates for the study. It was not clear in some cases whether patients could be designated as terminally ill. At other times, it was not clear whether the patient had been clearly told that his disease was incurable.

*12. Is it ethical to do research with terminally ill patients?* In this study terminal patients were not used for the sake of some research goal; rather, they were provided with high quality ministry on the part of the chaplains who at the same time invited patients to share information that might lead to a clearer understanding of patients in their situation. This is much the same as physicians who give the best care they can, while keeping careful records of the effects of new drugs and treatments. A patient was never asked to do anything against his will.

# Funerals: A Time for Grief and Growth

## Roy and Jane Nichols

*We have just explored the question of living until death—of what factors make this most possible. But what of living after death, of coping with the pain and shock that accompanies the death of a loved one? What factors contribute to those left behind learning to reinvest themselves in life? The selection that follows considers this issue.*

*When you think of a funeral and the preparation preceding it, what images come to mind?—a body artificially made-up to look "natural?" People being polite and insincere? Fighting back the tears because "it isn't mature to cry?" Hypocritical and meaningless services? Impersonal and uncaring persons? These are some of the typical responses most people have to funerals and all that surrounds them. Funerals have become, for many people, meaningless and uncomfortable rituals. But the Nichols paint us a moving and dramatic portrait of what a funeral should be—a time to say your last goodbys, to begin to work through your grief, to make death real through actively participating in the preparation and final service, to begin living again and growing through your experience.*

*As with many other things presented in this book, the reality of what works is the reverse of what we expect. We routinely shield the bereaved from coming face to face with the reality of the death of their loved one; we take over for them and invite them only to observe. And in doing this, we force them to submerge their grief, extending and expanding their pain and making it increasingly difficult for them to come to grips with the death. In the following selection, the authors offer an alternative to this kind of well-meaning deception. I only wish we could all be fortunate enough to find such loving, understanding human beings to help us when death comes to our families.*

Death and grief is man's curse or his glory, depending upon how he chooses to handle it.

On March 9, 1973, on my mother's birthday, my father died. I was holding his hand. He had had a stroke two years prior and another just one week before his death. My mother, my brother, and I sat on his hospital bed—powerless to help. I hated the scene, but I wouldn't have been anywhere else. I had a tremendous wish to stop the whole show, to run, to hide, to pretend it could not be. But dad's death was appropriate for his life. It was timely for him. What was happening was supposed to happen. I had to keep reminding myself of that. Such helplessness and desperation I have never felt at any other time. When he died, we wept.

Because I had been a funeral director for over ten years, because I was about sixty miles from my funeral home, and because the hospital preferred to have dad's body taken from the hospital promptly, I called a funeral director I knew from about three blocks away. I waited with dad.

Two men came with a cot—men I had never seen before. They didn't know me or my profession. My emotion didn't leave room for explanations, so I simply asked them to stand aside. It was my dad and I would do it. Hesitatingly they obliged while I took the cover from the cot, positioned the cot, and gathered dad's limp body into my arms. It was my job. I was his son. It was our love.

I felt a sense of desertion as I watched those two strangers disappear down the hall with dad. Dad didn't know them.

One of my best friends, a funeral director from the next town four miles from mine, came to get dad and did all the embalming work preparatory for the funeral. I did the rest—the death certificate, the notification of newspapers, cemetery, minister, church, family, friends, neighbors, all the scores of details which accompany the task of being a funeral director. Now I realize that I was functioning in a dual role, as a funeral director and as a son. I didn't need to be a funeral director, I needed to be a son; and I wanted to attend to the details myself—it was my dad, it was our love, it was my emotion, it was a son's job.

My mother, brother, sister, and I and our spouses found a high level of involvement in the succeeding days. We three kids had not been a closely knit family for several years; my sister living in California, my brother in New Jersey, and I in our native Ohio. But working through the many details and the sharing of responsibilities and feelings and togetherness renewed some of the childhood closeness. Dad would have been proud, probably is. Mom is proud.

Late in the evening the night before the funeral our minister, another close minister friend, and one of our favorite priests were, by coincidence, at the funeral home along with some thirty or forty friends. We had an impromptu prayer service—something which just happened. Thus gathered around in a circle, which included some flowers and dad's body in his casket, several of us shared our deepest feelings about dad's life and death and our own sense of mortality and immortality. It was very warming.

My family did lots of other things: we tucked dad in (it's rough but it's real) and closed his casket; we took him to church ourselves. My brother, sister, and I carried dad to his grave, we lowered him into his grave with straps and our own muscle power. We closed the vault and shoveled the dirt ourselves. We closed out his life ourselves.

I never asked dad who he wanted to have with him when he died. But if I had, I am certain he would have said, "The people I love the most." We were fortunate to be able to do almost all of it ourselves—for ourselves, for our needs, for our peace, and to get our grief work well started, immediately.

Later, weeks later, it dawned upon me what had happened and why it was all possible. As a funeral director, I had all the skills, tools, knowledge, and expertise at my fingertips. Whereas I functioned within the context of being a funeral director, I really was acting out my needs and responsibilities as a son. It was my job!! I simply could not allow strangers to be the functionaries.

But as a funeral director had I not been the functionary hundreds of times prior? How many other sons have been left in a void because I was a functionary for everything while they did little. In the personal experience of my father's death, my grief work started promptly because I had the opportunity to work through many of the last caring details of his death and funeral. I had had the opportunity to participate, to be involved on every level. How many sons, daughters, parents, and spouses had I delayed the grief work for because I had performed all of the tasks for them, because I, as a functionary, had usurped their role as care-giving family members. How many times had I made decisions for a family without their opinion, because I assumed "they couldn't take it?" They have a right to be heard. The focus must be on their needs, reactions, and prior experience. Immediately, my role in funeral service shifted to being that of a facilitator and it has remained there

As a facilitating funeral director I am free from imposing limits. I am open to those situations in which people need and want to be involved in the final opportunities to physically attend the significant family member or friend who has died.

Young people seem to seek out these opportunities the most. Perhaps it is because they have grown up in a generation in which death is an unknown. Perhaps it is because so much of their world is contrived and unreal. Perhaps it is because they have learned to throw off the shackles of materialism and seek personal, relevant, meaningful experiences. Perhaps it is because they have not had the benefit of prior realistic experience with death. For whatever reasons, they seem to want to be involved in the funeral experience.

Consider Butchie, a two year old boy who drowned in a neighbor's pond. The body was taken to the nearest hospital and the nineteen and twenty-two year old parents sat in a stunned shock staring into a cup of coffee and watching smoke curl from a cigarette.

Almost twenty-four hours later, a neighbor stumbled into the situation and we were summoned. We were aware that a great deal of the time during that initial meeting with Butchie's parents, their minds drifted. They were not with it; they could not believe it; they wished to be somewhere else. Struck by the severity of their denial and numbness and armed with what dad's death had taught us, we simply said, "When you bring Butchie's clothing to the funeral home, you tell us whether or not you want to dress Butchie's body. Don't tell us now, think it over and tell us then."

Three hours later they came and Carol stated that they wanted to dress their son. We sat on the floor and talked for quite awhile preparing them for what they wanted to do. It would hurt. So let it hurt. Someday they would understand, then it would be okay. But not today.

It took over two hours to dress Butchie. We stared, we swore, we cried, we talked, we apologized, we shared, we probed, we took time. Together, the four of us found our way through shock and disbelief, the beginning of emotional acceptance of what had happened.

When friends came, Carol and Charles were quite at ease with themselves, they had unloaded tremendous surges of emotion and were ready to receive the affection, concern, and support of their community. Shock, denial, and some hostility were behind them and their grief work was moving.

The funeral—those few days following a death—has many purposes. One of the most important purposes is to facilitate the grief work. Grief work begins with acceptance, with facing up. People need to come to grips with the reality of the death. This acceptance must not only be intellectual, it must also be emotional. What appears to be acceptance can be deceptive and can be very, very destructive when the acceptance is only intellectual.

When Russ died at age 43, swiftly and unexpectedly in Carol's arms in their home, Carol, who is an energetic, vivacious, and professional woman in her own right, tranquilized herself to avoid the pain. One professional caregiver set further tranquilization to the event with his advice, "We don't cry about these things, do we?"

She and her three children didn't. They were so brave, so strong. They braced themselves against the surges of emotion and sanctified their home so that Russ could live on with them. Some eighteen months after Russ's death, Carol called us in desperation. She was experiencing psychosomatic illness and sensations, she had suffered severe weight loss, she was unhappy and angry.

A visit to her home in a distant city found Carol in a blue dress, the home redecorated in a blue theme, and a blue car in the drive. Of course, blue was Russ's favorite color. His clothes were there, his shaving gear, his smoking apparatus, his easy chair; every room had his picture; the home was sanctified as a memorial to Russ.

"When will you let Russ die?" we inquired. "I don't want him to die," she replied. "But he is dead." "I know he is dead, but I don't want him to die." Intellectually, she knew his death had occurred; emotionally she denied it.

Her immediate, initial reaction of shock and denial had been prolonged into a destructive nightmare, because she had never taken the opportunity to actualize her loss. She had been tranquilized by a combination of medication, insensitive care-givers, and a death observance that permitted her denial. In eighteen months, she had been through three counselors, had been unable to maintain her job, but no one had gently and lovingly drawn her out of shock and denial into the real world.

Emotional acceptance takes time and work and pain and hurt. Care-givers, be they professional or laymen, often allow themselves to be trapped into trying to shield and protect the grieved from pain, only to extend and delay the pain to a later date. We cannot take the pain away. Whereas the grieved person may want withdrawal from reality (who wouldn't?), there is frequently a strong difference between what people want and what they need. We all must be aware of the extreme dangers of delayed, avoided grief and must develop the skills, the openness, the accepting attitude which will allow the grieved person to accept the death he has sustained. Participation in the funeral will facilitate that goal.

In an American society which is so defiant about death; which reveres youth so highly; which conceals the aged and the ill in institutions; which portrays death in the media as tragic, horrible, unlawful, unwanted, seldom as peaceful or wanted; which wants everything so comfortable and so convenient; which attempts to manipulate and control its total environment: in that kind of society death is frequently interpreted as an insult, an intruder, as unnecessary, as superimposed on life. The acceptance of death and the resulting ability to move through the grief work is severely inhibited by the notion that death cannot possibly be a part of the American Dream and the Good Life. As a result, our experience as funeral directors has revealed to us a strong tendency for people to withdraw from the death experience and to seek a functionary to perform the whole task. Yet our experience with dad's death revealed to us the benefits of moving closer to the death experience, of becoming a participant, rather than a spectator.

It's like the sport of football. One may be either a spectator or a player in the game. Spectators find their own level of involvement: some choose to stay at home and keep the game as an idea in the head, an intellectual concept; others choose to attend the game, but are preoccupied so that the game becomes a picnic in the park, a symphony concert, or whatever the mind is making it out to be; others sit passively and are content to observe; some are so sedated that they are scarcely aware that the game is being played; some keep themselves so busy buying hotdogs and visiting the rest rooms that they never know the score; some are as involved as the players, but they don't get the bruises. The players know the game best because they have studied, practiced, and prepared for the game. The players will have a greater awareness of the game and its outcome because they feel the pain of every blow.

And that's how it is with the response to death. Some attempt to keep it an intellectual concept, some are passive spectators, some active spectators, and some are players. Since the grief work depends upon the recognition of the game as being real and the willingness of the participants to be involved, it is likely that those who choose to get bruised by playing the game will have the greatest awareness of the reality of death and will come to understand their response to that death best.

People find their own level of involvement and should do so voluntarily. Never should a grieved person be forced into the role of participant or player. If he needs denial and withdrawal, it should be permitted, but he must also be aware of the consequences in terms of potential maladjustment and delayed grief reactions. The risks are heavy and serious. Emotions will be expressed either as an open healing wound or a closed festering wound, either honestly or dishonestly, either appropriately or inappropriately. But emotions will be expressed, and the grief work will be done.

Persons in grief have a whole jungle of emotions in their guts which need to be expressed in some way. Sometimes openly, sometimes by talking, sometimes by crying, sometimes poetically, sometimes through ritual: there are many ways, but people must have the opportunity to express real feelings because unresolved grief is a destructive horror.

People need to be encouraged to talk about the person who died, to remember him, to share about him, yes, perhaps to even talk to the person who is now dead.

When six-year-old Mary-Margaret died of a two year leukemia illness, her parents chose to wait with her in the hospital room until we arrived. With very few spoken words, we found that they wanted a high level of participation in her death and funeral. Mary-Margaret was their daughter, their love, their responsibility. Her father lifted her ravaged body and carried it to the cot. He pushed the cot through the corridors to the waiting car and lifted her into the car. Her mother asked to ride with Mary-Margaret to the funeral home. They spent a few hours alone with Mary-Margaret, with us, and with their minister. The next day Mary-Margaret's mother and maternal grandmother dressed her body and lifted it into the casket. After calling hours, when their friends had gone home, they sat with her for an extended period of time and talked to her and prayed for her. The next day they closed the casket and were the bearers. When we left for the church for the funeral service, they said, "We're ready . . . it's time now." We knew what they meant. They had come to a profound point of closure. They had made the transition, they were ready to give up her body, they had begun to remember, the pain was less now, and they could move on to seek meaning and understanding and to make their adjustment to life without her physical presence.

There is a movement in America to immediately dispose of the dead body at the time of death and to have a service without the body present which frequently attempts to focus on the qualities of the life of the dead person in an atmosphere of pseudo-calm and tranquility.

While this may be appropriate for expected death, it has been our experience in situations of sudden and unexpected death, childhood deaths, or expected death where the preparatory grief work is unfinished, that the grief needs of the survivors are frequently acute and a death observance that will promote the opportunity to actualize the loss, to express real feelings, and to feel community support will address itself more specifically toward the grief work. If the observance includes some level of involvement and participation among survivors, then it will facilitate and focus on the grief work. Anything else would be an insult and an abomination to the ultimate physical and mental health of the grieved persons and may set up the survivors for extreme difficulties in adjustment. The body, in our experience, is frequently the key to opening the door to the expression of honest and real feelings. The body, when properly used, is particularly helpful as a tool to getting the grief work well started and to doing it promptly.

Persons feel their needs in varying degrees of intensity and seek varying levels of involvement in the funeral. With permission, with gentle urging, with love, with interpretation, and while holding their hand, a high level of involvement can be achieved without disengagement. The outcome is gratifying. It is better for the voluntary involvement to be more than enough rather than to be less than enough. Because the death cannot be rehearsed at the emotional level and because it cannot be replayed later, it is vital in terms of adjustment needs to set a wise course and to make decisions which will facilitate the growth of the grieved person. The funeral is of value insofar as it embraces the sociological, psychological, and philosophical needs of those who lose a significant other.

Are needs met by avoidance or by spectatorship which permits denial? Or by hiring a functionary to do it all? Are needs really fulfilled by protecting from pain? Our choice isn't to avoid pain; our choice is only to permit pain to be experienced fast and hard or to be experienced slow and hard; that is our only choice.

One year old baby Keith, a mongoloid child, died in his parents' car while they were returning home from a week long vacation. Keith had caught a cold there and after consulting with their pediatrician, they started home. A swift invasion of pneumonia caused death to slam into Sue and Rob's lives, totally unexpectedly.

Our first meeting with Sue and Rob was for six hours while we listened to the purging of emotion; heard of the difficulties with police and physicians in a strange community who had investigated Keith's death, heard of the hostile reactions of wanting Keith to die when he was born fifty-three weeks ago (who wants a mongoloid child?); heard how they had counselled for months and studied mongolism and had grown to deeply cherish their Keith; how they were preparing to structure their home and marriage to raise a retardate. Then baby Keith died. How insulting! The guilt, the pain, the shame. To have wanted his death, to have learned how to love, to have wanted him to live, then to be faced with his death.

Rob and Sue asked for an intense level of involvement. Sue was over seven months pregnant. Fetus Two would soon be in their lives and Fetus One was suddenly dead. Sue and Rob had about six weeks to resolve their grief and get ready to love Fetus Two. Rob's professional job of managing a group of computer programmers necessitated his clear thinking, his ability to handle not only people, but also to keep volumes of data and information orderly. Rob could not afford to trip over suppressed emotions and feelings while running the office. Rob and Sue decided to unload the pain fast and hard.

The minister was especially selected for the specific task because he had a talent for speaking to the hurt. Rob and Sue made, for the funeral, a tape recording of personally meaningful folk music from their private collection of records. They chose to spend a whole morning with Keith's body—alone, before other people came. What they said, what they did, why they did it, only they and God and Keith know. But it helped. On the day of the funeral, after a very specific and skilled message by the minister, Rob and Sue closed Keith's little casket and held it in their laps as about forty friends went with them to the cemetery. They wanted honesty and realism so the grave was not concealed by artificial grass and the pile of dirt was not hidden. Rob and Sue, on their knees at the grave slowly, spontaneously, without any prior intent, placed Keith's body and casket into the grave and carefully began to pull dirt into the grave. The astute minister only said, "I think the kids need some help." Forty friends passed along the dirt, handful by handful, with no shovels, until the grave was filled. Then with dirt-caked hands, they heard the minister interpret to them what they had done, why they had done it, and what it meant to them.

In four days, Rob and Sue had reached closure with Keith's sudden death. They continue to affirm the value of their choice to take the pain hard and fast. They purposefully continue to deal with their emotions (it has been three months now) about Keith's life and death. Rob affirms that he is able to function well at work, free of the encumbrance of pent-up and repressed feelings. These young parents are growing because they are not shackled with inhibited grief work.

The ultimate goal of the grief work is to be able to remember without emotional pain and to be able to reinvest emotional surpluses. While the experience of the grief work is difficult and slow and wearing, it is also enriching and fulfilling. The most beautiful people we have known are those who have known defeat, known suffering, known struggle, known loss, and have found their way out of the depths. These persons have an appreciation, a sensitivity, and an understanding of life that fills them with compassion, gentleness, and a deep loving concern. Beautiful people do not just happen.

Growth can come in unexpected ways from the nooks and crannies of our life's experiences. In death and in grief we do not need as much protection from painful experiences as we need the boldness to face them. We do not need as much tranquilization from pain as we need the strength to conquer it. If we choose to love, we must also have the courage to grieve.

What a blessing to take the time to pause from our well-meant efficiency as professionals and as layman to care, to gentle, to share, to listen, to feel, to respond to each other and to ourselves. What a blessing to take the time to integrate loss into our lives so that when a love is lost, our capacity to love is not lost also. From our grief can come growth.

# A Mother Mourns and Grows

## Edith Mize

*One of the hardest kinds of death to accept is that of one's child. "You wonder why not me, why him?" It's a rude reminder that death follows no predictable timetable, but chooses its own time and place. Painful though this experience is, it can also be an impetus to growth for those who accept the challenge. There are two choices when a loved one dies—to live in grief, remorse, and guilt covered thinly by façade; or to face those feelings, work them through, and emerge with an acceptance of death and a commitment to living.*

*One of the ways that many parents I know whose children have died use to work through their grief is writing down their feelings. Many times we can write what we cannot speak aloud or otherwise formulate into concrete thoughts that we can then deal with. On the following pages Edith Mize shares, in chronological order, some of the conversations she had with her critically ill son prior to his death at age 26; they reflect her struggle through the stages from shock and denial to acceptance. Then we see her continued growth as she uses writing after his death as a means to work through her grief and begins to live again, now with a renewed sense of purpose.*

*These selections are the writings of a mother, suffering and struggling, who found in writing a vehicle through which to express and deal with her own inner pain. She has gone through grief and mourning—not yet finished—yet it is in her sorrow that she has become creative, and it is out of her tears that she found words of beauty and love.*

### Shock

(February 15) After his operation:
"Why did this happen to me?"

RON

---

*Denial*
"This can't be true. He will get better."

MOTHER

*Anger* (an expression to relieve the anguish)
(March)
"I don't want these Get Well Cards."

RON

*Hope*
"There's hope, don't give up now. Many things are being done to help you."

MOTHER

*Isolation*
"Stop phoning me all the time or I'll change my phone number."

RON

"But I worry about you, and you don't phone back."

MOTHER

*Bargaining*
(April 27th)
"Happy Birthday to Ron and Lisbet." (We had a small party).
I prayed for a miracle and could not let go.

MOTHER

Ron went to California (his favorite state) for a two weeks vacation and to visit with friends.
(May 7th)
My birthday. I was happy he was still with us.

MOTHER

"Stop acting like Pollyanna. I don't have tonsillitis."

RON

"There's some hope. Please, don't give up yet."

MOTHER

*Anger* (frustration)
(June)
"Why am I working so hard repairing my Volkswagen? I can't use it in Heaven."

RON

"But think of all the experience you have gained!"

MOTHER

*Anger*
(June)
"Ron, you'll not die of cancer, but a concussion. You're making me angry. Think positive. I can't let you go now."

MOTHER

He laughed and said, "Okay, you never give up."

RON

"Right on!"

MOTHER

*Depression* (facing reality)
(July 13 (Friday at home))
"Let go of me. I will not live like this. I can't take this pain; the weakness; and I'm tired of fighting."

RON

"If you have too much pain and there's no more hope I will let you go."

MOTHER

"Good, let's go on the boat. I'm tired of hanging around the house. I'm going fishing."

RON

"Okay. That's a good idea."

MOTHER

*Depression* (a normal reaction)
"I can't take these treatments anymore. I won't be a guinea pig and the treatments don't help. They make me ill."

RON

"Please try because everyone loves you."

MOTHER

(July 27th) (A visit to the hospital)
"Not yet, Ron." (but I knew)

MOTHER

"I wish they would tell me what's wrong. They had a consultation about me, but I wasn't invited."

RON

*Acceptance*

(August 3) (a final stage and a peaceful one)
Last visit to Ron in the hospital.
"I have a slight headache. I won't be having much pain anymore."

RON TO HIS FRIEND, TOM

*Acceptance*

(August 5) (Sunday)
Ron was comatose and sleeping quietly.
"Goodbye, Ron, God Bless you. I love you so much."
It was better for him, and I finally let go. I did not want him to suffer.

MOTHER

The dying patient's problems cease, but the family must live on. They then cope with grief. If one is prepared for the death (anticipatory grief) it helps. Eventually the family learns to live with the loss. There is no time limit on grief. One cannot know "why" but continues to live. The death of a young adult is hard to accept.

## GRIEF

When someone you love dies, you have a feeling of numbness; a yearning; and a protest. You have lost part of yourself; you feel disorganized; and you do much crying. You're restless, and you may feel guilty. Perhaps you could have helped the one who died but you do not know how. You are angry because the person died, and you are angry at the world. You feel so alone, and loneliness is one of the biggest problems of grief. It is your problem and you have to solve it alone.

The first stage of grief is shock, and it helps temporarily. A grieving person is not overwhelmed by the tremendous loss of the loved one immediately after the death. There are many things to do and you do them automatically. I kept very busy and tried not to think that Ron was gone. I could not believe that he was gone and hoped for a better tomorrow.

Soon I realized our only son was gone and religious faith could not help me. I looked for answers and there were none. I kept thinking "What will I do without him? I miss him." People react to grief in different ways. I have the need to believe that my son exists somewhere but I do not know where. Will I see him again? I do not know but hope I will. My belief is based on my emotional need and not on my reasoning.

As I progressed through the stages of grief, I had the usual psychosomatic symptoms; my body ached and the emotional tension was getting to me. I could not sleep and was tired. I had pushed myself while he was ill for the six months, and his death affected me greatly. My optimistic attitude vanished when he died.

At times after his death I was absentminded; felt panicky; and did not function the way I wanted to. I know the various stages of grief are normal, but unless you know this you think something is wrong with you.

I had a few guilt feelings and thought as a registered nurse I should have realized our son had cancer. There was no way I could have known. He did not complain about feeling ill and cancer slowly attacked his body. Guilt is a common reaction for a grieving person.

I also felt angry about many things. He was too young to die but who is to know when it is the right time to die? For some unknown reason it was his time. I do not know why it had to be now.

Grief cannot be hurried, but eventually an emotional balance returns to the grieving person. You cannot bring back the one you love but you have to face reality. A change has occurred in my life, and my life must now have more meaning. I watched our son fight to live and stood by as he accepted death. He knew there was not much hope for him and became very brave. I could not disappoint him and I had to be strong for him.

My grief consumes me at times but I will learn to live with my loss. I cannot forget our son, and for now his death is too much for me to comprehend. However, I have to continue on. It takes time to reduce grief. I am trying to move forward. Our son would not want me to spend most of my time grieving for him. He always told me to "forge ahead," and I will make the effort for him. I will do whatever I can to the best of my ability. It seems such a loss for someone as vital as Ron to be gone. When death strikes it is a terrible blow and the pain is tremendous. I know it takes time to heal a painful wound, especially one affecting your heart. I cannot give up and I am trying to make my life significant.

## TO THE DOCTOR

Do you know how it feels
 As one is dying?
Can you relate to someone
 Who is crying?
Look at the person
 Who depends on you
Who needs your strength
 And compassion too.

A person who's now so ill
 His life may soon be gone;
He needs your help; ease his pain
 As he lingers on;
He needs stamina and courage
 To fight his fight,
Perhaps may not make it
 Through the long night.

Do what you can for him each day
 You know he is trying,
As he looks at the unknown.
 He knows he is dying.
He wants so much to live
 To him it is unfair;
Let him know you're nearby,
 Let him know you care.


## ACCEPTANCE

Why is one sad
When it's time to die?
It's because he's leaving
And that's why he cries.

It's not he's afraid
Afraid of what?
It's because of what
He's about to give up.

Onward and upward
Look for the light
Try not to despair
It will be all right.

As one is dying
He thinks about life
Both are a battle
But worth the fight.


## TRY AGAIN

I'm tired of gloom;
I'm tired of pain;
I want to rejoin
The world again.

Life does proceed
When a loved one leaves
But it's difficult for me
Who is left to grieve.

Today I will try
To smile once more.
Death disappeared
And left my door.

I'll pick myself up
And try again;
I'll make the effort
To function again.

It won't be easy
As I well know,
But I won't give up
The change made me grow.

I loved him so much,
And fate was unkind.
He went away first;
He left me behind.

The pain in my heart
Will remain for awhile
But yesterday's gone
Today I will smile.

What is a meaningful life and who can explain death? There are no available answers. The answers are within a person. Whatever makes you content and secure in life—that is the answer to the question of existence. Ambition, goals to achieve, and hope in the future make life worth living.

I can accept the fact that I will die someday, but it was difficult to accept the fact our only son was dying at an early age; however, he accomplished many of his goals. I had to let go of him when there was not much hope.

I wish he had talked to me more about life and death because he knew he was dying. It is upsetting for a terminally ill patient to discuss death with one he loves and especially with his mother. We were very fond of each other, and I will always miss him. He enjoyed living and had to accept the tribulation of death. Towards the end he realized I could accept the fact he was leaving us. He was brave and I had to be also. I am glad his father, sister, friends, and I were with him. He had a peaceful death and did not die in vain.

Many people have donated money in his memory (to the hospital) and it will be used for research and I am grateful. For Ron to live on in memory for a worthy cause is something I am proud of. I am sure he would be very surprised. He meant so much to so many people and did not realize it. Sometimes we are so busy living that we forget to let others know how much we care, and we take too much for granted. I am guilty of this also.

If my writing makes you stop and think about life and death, and gives you some insight, then I have accomplished something in a small way. I know our son's death made my life more meaningful . . . may he rest in peace and I will continue to have "the will to believe."

# One Woman's Death—
# A Victory and a Triumph

## Dorothy Pitkin

*The final word on the quality of death and of life lies with the dying person. It is ultimately the one who is dying who determines what note his or her life will end on—whether death will be the culmination of a lifetime well lived or merely the end of a number of years spent in this world. Our final lessons about death have to come from the patient. I chose Dorothy Pitkin's last writings—not so much because of what it expresses about death, because death is really not its subject; but rather, because of what it has to say about living. They give us a view of the end of a life stripped by circumstances of dignity and meaning, and at the same time a portrait of a woman who refuses to relinquish her humanness. I never met Dorothy Pitkin, yet I feel very close to her. She was a hard worker, a mother, a writer, but most of all perhaps, a fierce fighter for life. Her son writes: ". . . she never gave up, yet at the end she died with great serenity and dignity. We felt strongly that her burial underneath the light house of Monhegan Island and the services we had for her should reflect that affirmative and rebellious character." Perhaps the main reason why I chose to include her writings is that she represents a woman of fantastic internal strength; she was not to be defeated and dehumanized, but was able to grow—she died "a big woman" though, who knows, she may have been only five feet tall. In the end we are always alone, but it is not the number of people who surround us in our dying, nor is it the number of years that we have lived that is significant; it is the quality of life and the courage and strength we have shown that ultimately gives us the strength to face this final journey alone and with dignity. Her son's letter describes her philosophy and her death, followed by Dorothy Pitkin's last writings.*

Dorothy was seventy-five-years old and weighed eighty pounds

"One Woman's Death—A Victory and a Triumph," by Dorothy Pitkin, edited by R. C. Townsend. Originally titled "The Cold Literal Moments," © 1974 by The Massachusetts Review, Inc. Reprinted by permission of the Massachusetts Review.

when she died, but "Dorf" was never old. She refused to be an old lady, and even the role of grandmother was not a comfortable one for her. She was best with her children when they were people in their own right. Childhood with Dorothy for a mother was not easy. She was a powerful person, and you had to work hard to win your own core of being against such force. But she saw to it that her children's imagination would be respected and stimulated by providing them with the tools and freedom to explore their own worlds of imagination. She responded with enthusiasm to our enthusiasms. She was lucky to marry a man who adored her and respected her independence. They loved the life of the country and shared an appreciation of simple enjoyments. But, for Dorothy, marriage and family were not enough, and we all knew with some pain that we were not the center of her life.

In the beginning was the word, and the word was God. The word was Dorothy's touchstone. Writing was her anchor. It was both a terrible tyranny and her sole liberation. She was chained to her typewriter like Prometheus to his rock and yet it was her universe, her garden. Writing was both her art and her religion. Two weeks before she died she sat for the last time before her typewriter. She missed hardly a day of her life in its intimate presence. When she could no longer type in these weeks, she wrote notes in the margin of any books at hand, or on stray scraps of paper. They were prayers. They all said the same thing, "Dear God, help me to find the way." It would be too easy to say that she found the way, but she had always set her course by the North Star and she never deviated from it. Dorothy had a dream of a place that was right, her refuge, and the North Star pointed to it. She had always hoped to find it, as she said, by turning a coin on the other side.

Early on, Dorothy ate from the fruit of knowledge and was cursed by the knowledge that life was not as convention decreed. She celebrated life's terrible beauty. Her awareness cost her her complacency and even that degree of quietude that she sought for herself. A quietude that she always felt Henry David Thoreau promised her. Thoreau was for a long time her guru and reaffirmed Dorothy's conviction that life spent in the pursuit of respectability and materiality was an illusion. She was a yea sayer to life. She was our guru. And yet Dorothy did win her share of success as this world counts it. She would have liked her obituary titling her as an author and actress. Her four books were a source of pride, yet were always dismissed by her as a mere approximation of what she wanted to say, of what she must say.

Fear was a constant companion of her life. The fear that is the companion of all those who are aware of the hurt of life, its absurdities, and its beauty. That apprehension is the stuff from which all art, poetry, and discovery come. It is the antithesis of complacency. She never made plans for her own death, she never resigned herself to it, she never even philosophized about it. She felt to do so would have been a cop out from life. Even the last few days when life had given her up, she continued to affirm it, and to believe in her recovery. But deep inside she knew full well she was going to die.

On Monday the nurse called to say that Dorothy's day had come. That morning we played eye games together, and she waved "ciao" with her hands. We sang "Jesus Christ Superstar" for her—she loved that music. She waited for Jane to arrive from Vermont to join Don, Steve, Roxie, and Ann. We held her hands and she died with grace and dignity.

## DOROTHY PITKIN'S FINAL WRITINGS

Now I must begin again. I must begin with a new woman, with the one who goes to the Nursing Home.

It is evening and I have the lonesome feeling that I am far from home but I do not know where home is. Being in a Nursing Home. My roommates are at the movies, something or other from Hawaii. They are in their wheelchairs and one or two of them have the special dress they must wear at evening affairs. A little old and old fashioned.

They come wheeling into the rotunda and make a circle with all the chairs. Some fancy hand wheeling, jockeying into place. I am impressed with the professional way the women handle their machines.

They are before the big window watching the evening turn slowly into night. Then the dark bands remain, after the dying of the evening. This meeting of the women trying to pay tribute to the evening. A special evening meeting. Watching the evening come on, and the flowering of the evening. The flowering of the lights. Blue, green or red.

I, the new woman, watch the sky and feel the potency of the evening. Thinking where I have watched the sun set before.

Here I was one morning. I was alone on the "Porch" sitting in my wheelchair and the moment was mine. It might not be the moment of truth, but it was mine, and the moment could be anything I might want it to be. There had been several old houses I had lived in when I was a child, and I had loved every blade of grass in their gardens. Before me the broad sweep of new cut grass stretched away to the tall uncut grass, and the bushes and the trees that crowded the hillside. In the spring the uncut grass was shiny with little drops of dew, but now it was fall and the tall grass was bent and brown. I loved every blade of grass, cut or uncut, but now there was sadness in my looking. It was not my grass. Everything I saw was beautiful, but it belonged to the Nursing Home. I could not see it as I wished to see it. It was not my grass. I was not a free person, not a whole person. My day was scheduled according to the Nursing Home's demands. I belonged to the Nursing Home and everything I saw was theirs.

Before I went as a patient to the Nursing Home Monastery, I lived in a small apartment nearby. My windows overlooked the yard and I could see people, patients, entering, sometimes via the wheel chair ambulance, sometimes supported by nurses' aides. It had never occurred to me that someday I might be living there.

It sits on the top of a small hill. Its members belong to a special universe. It is known simply as the Nursing Home. I first said Monastery. I wish it was. All men. I can deal with men. They do not have to answer a lot of questions such as what dress do you want to wear today? How about your hair? Shall we make it a la Marie Antoinette? Before she lost her head, of course. Men can stay right in their chairs while nurses look here and there, not for little scarlet ribbons to tie around Jim Palmer's bald head, but for such things as old hunting caps and tin firemen's hats which become them very well. Altogether, bald or with hair, they have an easier time of it than women do at the Nursing Home Monastery.

But I am a woman and everything gets mixed up here. I have no compass. No guiding finger points the way for me to go. I ask myself what in God's name am I doing here, alone, and so far away from home—wherever that may be, I am not quite sure. They will tell you I am here because I am old. I have forgotten the feelings that belong to youth, but sometimes the feelings that belong to youth come swimming up from the deep blue. Then I know that I have not forgotten those feelings. They belong to me even though I am old. One day, I looked up not down. A mountain of a man loomed over my chair. "Want a workout?" "Yes?" "Right now?" "Good girl." Through some miracle of levitation, I rise, pulled up by one arm of the mountain and stand on my feet, and there is the physiotherapist, better than a mountain, a man. "Now, you walk, walk, you walk."

Heels first, and then your toes. Heels, toes, heels, toes. And this happens five days of the week. "Am I doing any better?" "Better than what?" "You're doing all right." "You know any better way?" "You'll just have to walk, walk." "That's it." "Remember, you're not a teenager." "You're doing alright for an old dame." "You don't like that, do you." "Well after all there was this Madam something or other. She weighed two hundred and ten pounds, and she was one hundred and twenty years old, but she sailed down the wind like a bird on the wing. That should give you confidence. Well now, what do you say, shall we, to coin a phrase, put the show on the road?" "Yes." "I didn't hear you, speak up, don't mumble. Is it yes or no?" "Yes." "Do you mean YES?" "YES!" I shout. "Well, that's better, it's yes, right? You mean YES, yes?" Every statement in the Nursing Home Monastery must be repeated at least eight times. "You want to go to the bathroom. You want to go to the bathroom. You want to go to the bathroom. You mean you want to go to the bathroom. You mean you want to go to the bathroom." With every statement the tone of voice rises higher, and becomes more nasal. I hear it now, you don't want to go to the bathroom, right? Right! Well why didn't you say so in the first place. Well, what do you say, shall we put the show on the road? Right? Right. I mean no. Oh, I don't know what to say. No. Yes. Right. No. Right. Right. You don't want to go to the bathroom, is that it? Right? No. Right? Well then, shall we put the show on the road, right? NO. Right! Yes. No. Yes. No. Yes! Right! Right!

Now I start with waking to the day, with the big window showing the sky, the dawn colors in the big window. From my bed the whole sky is seen. The birds wheeling across the sky. Hawks with the sharp, incised wings. A sort of message from the sky. I lie here and look at the sky. Then the morning cry, the cry, breakfast? The trays are up. And I pull on a colored robe to sit in my chair and have my breakfast. "Trays are up" comes the cry from the kitchen. My cue to get ready. Swing my legs over the side and struggle up to sit on the edge of the bed. Soon the young nurse's aide sails in like a dancer bearing the tray aloft. She sets it on the bedside table. "Good morning!" "Here you go." "Eat your breakfast." "Here is your toast and your cereal." "Here is your prune juice." "Drink it all, it is good for you." My prune juice, I think. They insist on calling it my prune juice but it certainly is not *my* prune juice. I'll drink it under protest. The nurses aide is pretty and young in her white clothes, and gayly maternal. Her skirts end far above the knee. "Now be a good girl and eat a good breakfast for me." And not for me, I think. The pretty girl opens the little packets of sugar. "Here is your coffee and your milk and here is your buttered roll." "All set?" "Okay?" But usually it is just, "Kay?" "Kay?" "Okay, now be a good girl and eat it all up." "Kay?" "Okay?" And off she sails to get Mrs. Pitchares' tray, and Mrs. Ogelthorpe's, and Mrs. Murphy's, and Mrs. Wetmore's tray with a "Kay?" and a firm final "Okay." Birds are flying high.

After breakfast comes the first of the long, long waits. This one occurs when I am a long time sitting precariously on the edge of the bed, waiting, waiting, to begin the morning's bathing. Finally the nurse appears with a basin. "You can wash yourself here and brush your teeth too." "Do as much as you can." "I will be in to do your back." "Just ring when you are through and I will come." Somehow I manage to wash myself, without slipping over the edge of the bed. I ring the little bell and wait and wait and wait for the nurse to come. I cannot see my clock but it must be many minutes that I wait and wait, naked, sitting in great discomfort on the edge of the bed. Having no privacy is my main trial. I sit feeling very naked and hoping I may get dressed before the maintenance man comes in pushing a mop around. This is usually the time for the first of the maintenance men to appear picking up stray rubbish from the floor. "Good morning!" "Good morning to you." "How are you today?" "Pretty good." "That's good!" He seems to be quite unconscious of the little glimpse he has of the naked woman through the curtains that don't quite come together. After he has gone, again I wait and wait for someone, anyone to come. Finally the curtain is pulled back and someone I have never seen before appears. "Can I help you?" "Get washed and dressed!" "Okay?" "I'll be back in just a minute." Out she rushes and doesn't come back. Finally another nurse's aide appears. "What's the problem?" "Get washed and dressed!" "Okay?" And the miracle happens. She doesn't go out but gets down to business. There and then she helps me to get washed and dressed.

First breakfast and washing and dressing. And then perhaps I might be present at a lecture on the Grand Canyon. Or Toledo in the fall or maybe Quebec. The patients sit in rows and there is always the question, can you see? How about if we pushed your wheel chair next to Mrs. Barabee. There, is that better?? Can you see now? These are very interesting pictures. Especially the one on Toledo. There now is that better?? Sure you can see around that post? Look, if you turn your head a little, you can see at least half of it. That's the spirit! Seeing half of it is better than not seeing anything at all. The pictures were lurid in color—a green face, another one purple. If Toledo looked like this you would certainly not want to go there. Around me the other patients were growing restless. I watched April with envy in her wheel chair. The best thing about wheel chairs was the ability to get out of here. April handled her wheel chair with swift ability. Look at her, getting out of here!

Robert Frost said it. Home is where you don't want to go because they have to take you there when you are ill or old and there is no other place to go. Nowadays the Nursing Home takes you. And the best of the Nursing Homes have modern methods of rehabilitation such as physiotherapy. Here are not just old people marking time until the end. Here the battle against age is being fought.

First, you get up and out of bed. You get washed and dressed. Then, what shall we work on today? Rising from a chair. A stretching exercise. Going up and down stairs. But most important, walking, walking because you must function and walking is the basis of all this. But when you cannot walk because of broken hips, or missing a leg, or even two, it is still movement, going from here to there. Overcoming the limitation by means of a wheel chair, or such a device as walkers. Exercises which strengthen worn muscles help to coordinate joints and muscles. Becoming independent, this is the pole star they guide themselves by. Here is something known as going up and down stairs. A terrifying experience. Here we go on nightmare stairs. A flight of stairs that might take you to a dungeon. My God, how can I do this? Why should I do it? Because the stairs are there, and you must do this. Hold on to the rail on your side, and keep coming, let your arm keep in time with your feet. There you are at the bottom, and now you must turn around and come on back. And here you are, you have reached the top of the stairs.

Stand up Mary, stand up on your feet. Talk to your feet. See? Oh this is beautiful. If you stand up on your feet, you will not fall on your face. Mary is held up by two helpers. Mary you can walk, try. I am trying. This is what many helpers do not understand. They think if you would only try, you can stand up on your feet. And here is Mary trying desperately to stand. Held by two workers, her face distorted in desperate urgency, I can't, I can't, I am trying to! Talk to your feet Mary, tell them to move. I can't. Half dragged on feet that half walked and tried to meet the floor, she reaches the chair.

Right now, let us take a look at some of the members of this special universe. Let us start with Jean. I wish you could see her walking, just walking, a big woman, with a big face that somehow is a little girl's face. She bends upon you that little girl's face that has been her face since she was twelve. Her dress is a little girl's dress. Or it might be doll's clothes, and she is the doll. Someone wound her up and set her going, and she walks up and down and down and up always with a dignified measured pace, not slow, not fast. Lately her hair has been growing in a thick mass at the back of her head. The little girl's face is lost and she looks like a buffalo with that hump of hair at the back of her head, walking, just walking, still with that steady, measured pace, a buffalo that has lost its way and is trying to get back to the pack.

Here is Leo without any legs. His body ends close to his face. He has dignity and authority bringing wisdom. He has a man's smile that is far more male than many another male blessed with the good fortune of legs. Leo is tough. He is all man. Better not offer sympathy to Leo. He stands alone, not seeking anything from anyone. He goes in his chair to sit in the sun, all day. He is alone but there he is a figure without legs taking command of the great field beside the river, alone but not lonely.

Now here comes Teddy in his wheelchair. There must have been some physical malfunction at the time of his birth. Or perhaps some miscarriage of the constellations. He cannot walk. He cannot talk, except with strange sounds that an animal might make, trying with desperate urgency to make himself understood. He wheels his chair close to the woman who makes the paper bunnies and peers at them with a pixy look on his strange yellow face. What is this? He turns his hands outwards in his usual way to emphasize what he has said. Always this gesture asks the world to translate what goes on in this place. He could be the director or chief character actor bringing meaning which has no meaning in the theater of the absurd.

And there is little Martha, sitting on the commode in full sight of everyone coming in. Not even a curtain drawn. She sits there in full sight of everyone. Not even behind a door. Sitting there in full view of everyone, right in the middle of the room, granted no privacy. The commode in the middle of the room. It would be just as easy as setting the chair in the bathroom. This is the exact middle of the room. A callous disregard of privacy. Almost as though they picked out the most public place to sit there before everyone. As public as anyone can be. For Martha there is the clock. The clock is the center of the universe. She looks into its face with tender recognition. I wish people could see Martha's beauty and the sadness that is in her face. A seeking that underlies the resignation, an understanding of the rejection of the clock and the "no" to herself. The clock must be with her day and night. When bedtime comes she must have the clock where she can see it, the guardian angel of her sleep. Two clocks have been dropped and broken. Oh God, my clock, how can I sleep without it. I must have my clock! I must hear my clock tick when I need it. When I held it to my ear it ticked. Now here is the third clock and when I hold it to my ear it ticks. A miracle of time!

Fear has many faces. What is this that binds us and will not let us go? Jean has it and sits in the dark room they call the dining room where she bows her head upon the table and has dreams she cannot understand. Jim has it too, walking here and there with a face full of great misery, his toothless mouth a great cavern. He is looking for his children. "Where are my children?" "Where is, where is she?" He puts out a hand to stop the passerby. "Mister, listen, Mister, have you seen my children, have you seen my daughter Agnes? I am Jim Campbell. You must know Jim Campbell. I ran the paper mill. I am looking for my children. Have you seen them? They were here but they have gone away."

There is a time between the dark and dawn when feet are heard hurrying and the sound of crying echoes through the passages of night. Mary is awake. Mary is crying. Mary it is night, and you must sleep. When morning breaks it will be, Mary, it is morning and you must stand up straight on your feet. Now it is night and you must roll over, close your eyes and go to sleep.

They are settling Joe in his wheel chair. Joe is Polish and he swears in Polish because they have taken from him his manhood. He has become a naughty child to be petted and spanked and stuck in a wheel chair. His skinny legs that stick out of the wheel chair do not belong to him any more. They belong to the Nursing Home Monastery, and they must do what they tell him to do because he is no longer a man.

Some fears are worse than others. But getting old underlines all they may say or do. Head up, shoulders straight, all set, and there you are, ready to go.

But the trouble is that you are not ready to walk. How different this is from the way it used to be when the little apartment near the woods was home. There, rising from a chair was a graceful thing, almost a dance, slow time. Now getting to my feet is a bitter thing, and I know no one wants to watch my struggle. Moreover, I know they do not want to be seen with a woman who must use a thing called a walker to rise and walk. This is a hospital case. It is not for them.

Now morning breaks. From this bed there is nothing to be seen except the deep blue with surprise colors like banners across the sky.

When the pain gradually takes over, fear lies with me and the stale old memories come back.

I was twenty years older than he was. At first he was my student in the Photography Department at the college. He was then twenty years old and that would make me forty at that time. I was well known as a photographer of all the important happenings, he took my classes, and I became interested in his way of seeing things. He was direct and objective, not trying to make the oblique, the super dramatic angle. For instance, at the time of the mine cave in, when men were trapped in the pocket of the mine, I would take a dramatic thing of it, like the faces of the relatives showing them contorted with fear, or something like a small child crying, or maybe the red jacket left behind the trapped in place. This he accepts as a way of showing the devastation, he accepts it as a way of showing the meaning of the experience, from a subtle way of doing it. He says, yes this is interesting. Always the off beat angle. He is with it, he says. He agrees with me, but never takes it over entirely. I am aware of his nonacceptance, unspoken, but there it is. One day I become outspoken, in my annoyance . . . "Look, you might be my son. I can ask you, why do you not come right out and tell me what you object to, it would be better if you came right out and say you do not like it, as you would if you were really my son." "Your son? Listen, I am not your son. You know how I feel about you. I am definitely not your son." And suddenly it happens. He tilts my head up and kisses my cheek. "This is the way a son would greet his mother. And this is the way I feel about you." Suddenly his lips are pressed with passion on my lips. "We may as well face it right now, you are not my mother. I am not your son." "Yes Mother? Is this right, Mother?" Always the slight mockery, implied in everything he says or does. But now it comes out in the open. He is a lover. He never says lover, he shows how he feels by the passionate kiss, mouth on mouth. "Tell me, is this how you feel about me" he asks through the kiss, his mouth pressed passionately on my mouth. "Yes? Yes?" "Tell me yes." And I feel the passionate flood of feeling rush over me. He is not a son but a lover. "Yes," I whisper through the kiss, his mouth on mine. "Yes," I whisper helplessly. "And it has always been this way? Say yes." "Yes," I whisper with his teeth pressed on mine.

There was that walk which we took through the beech woods, and after that nothing was the same. Then it all came out—what we had both been hiding or rather we acknowledged the feeling we had always had. The beech woods had a small brook running along the middle. When we came to the dense part of the woods, he said, "Take a step towards the right of the brook. Never mind the rocks and stones, I have a hold of you." It seemed to me he had chosen the worst part of the brook. "Come on, you can do it Mother." The "Mother" came out in a tone of sarcasm though he had used "Mother" before. We had used it kiddingly before. I once told him I thought of him as a son. "I have never had a son, now you can be one." That was when I was correcting one of the papers I had given him to do. A summary of what photography comprises today. "It is an art, and you must employ it as an art. Take the most significant parts of the picture and make what you can of them. That is the way it is done, son." And it was then that we jumped over the brook. And the beech woods walk became the symbol of our relationship. Son, lover, lover, son . . . Now a lover.

Now in the Nursing Home, I see him so clearly. The way he looked when we jumped over the brook and the way he looked when he tilted my face to kiss my cheek and the passionate face when he kissed my mouth, and I thought things will never be the same. This is my lover. Now that I am in the Nursing Home, I see him so clearly, the male blond hair, his skin smooth as a woman's, but the male mouth, and his blue eyes. Some might say a killer's blue, sharp and clear, but a lover's blue too. Maybe the two went together, the killer's blue, and the lover's blue.

Now when I wake at the Nursing Home, I remember how I used to wake in the little apartment near the beech woods. I would wake and think something good is going to happen today. Then the happiness would steal over me. He is coming today. And I will set the table with the red and white tablecloth. And set the candles in the Italian candle holders. And the cheese will be provolone and oh yes, the wine will be Liebfraunmilch, the wine he likes. Today there is going to be a celebration as today he is going to be forty, twenty years younger than me. And often before I would think twenty years younger. Now he is thirty and I am fifty, and this is the way it will always be, I am twenty years older than he.

We were sitting in the room in twilight. This was how we liked to sit, no lights yet. The evening light fell on his hair and it was a soft male blond.

After dinner we talked about this business of older? Younger? And how it affected our relationship. You might think it was something indecent, for a woman, to be twenty years older than the man she loved. Probably it belonged to the Victorian days, when a woman was supposed to need the support of the man she loved. She was supposed to be weaker than the male, in need of help in everything she did or did not do. The man must be older than the woman to give her that support.

But here there is no support. There is nothing I can do but survive. The time is at the turning. Evening is turning into night. The arc of the sky is filled with great bands of sunset. Birds are flying high. It is a lonely time for me. I feel lost and far away from home. But where is home? I have never found it.

My roommates come wheeling into the room with many windows to watch the evening bands of color turn slowly into the dark shapes of night. About eight o'clock they begin to consult their watches. I have a quarter to eight, but I may be wrong. No, it is fifteen past seven but my watch may be wrong. What do you make of it? Call it seventeen to eight. That is closer to it. I feel the hurt that steals over me. It is a stealthy oncoming, this potency of night.

So after the supper had been cleared away, I stepped out into the night. My night. It was black night and the stars were my stars, I was alone with them. It was so still, the only sound was the tide coming, coming in, coming in. It was a pulse. It was there, it never stopped. It said be still and know that I am here. The timing of the pulse was the timing of my pulse. So I am the child of the tide.

# 5
# Death and Growth: Unlikely Partners?

How can death contribute to growth, either in the one who dies or in those who are left behind? Our conventional views of death bring to mind many thoughts and feelings, but they rarely include the prospect of growth. And yet, we have seen from our discussion that if we look at death from a different perspective, then we can see that it is the promise of death and the experience of dying, more than any other force in life, that can move a human being to grow. All of us, even those who have chosen a life of non-growth—of playing out the roles prescribed by others—feel within our innermost selves that we are meant for something more in this life than simply eating, sleeping, watching television, and going to work 5 days a week. That something else, that many can't define, is growth—becoming all that is truly you and at the same time, more fully human.

Strange though it may seem to you, one of the most productive avenues for growth is found through the study and experience of death. Perhaps death reminds us that our time is limited and that we'd better accomplish our purpose here on earth before our time runs out. Whatever the reason, individuals who have been fortunate enough to share in the death of someone who understood its meaning seem better able to live and grow because of their experience. Those who have been immersed in the tragedy of massive death during wartime, and who have faced it squarely, never allowing their senses and feelings to become numbed and indifferent, have emerged from their experiences with growth and humanness greater than that achieved through almost any other means.

Death can be very hard to face, and we might be tempted to avoid it and flee from having to confront it. But if you have the courage to deal with it when it comes into your life—to accept it as an important and valuable part of life—then, whether you are facing your own death, that of someone in your care, or that of a loved one, you will grow.

In my book *On Death and Dying*, I describe the stages that human beings typically go through in their experience of dying. These stages—denial, rage and anger, bargaining, depression, and acceptance—are briefly reviewed in Dr. Mauksch's piece in chapter II. Although a sensitive, feeling human being will not (and should not) ever be immune to feelings of sadness, even despair and depression, on the death of a loved one; nevertheless you *can* become more at peace with the thought of death and more able to deal with it in a productive way if you are able to go through the experience with others. As they go through the stages of dying, if you share their experience, you also will be brought increasingly closer to a level of acceptance yourself. (Clearly, not everyone who is dying ever reaches a level of acceptance, but if you can do so *before* you are faced with your own or a loved one's death, then you will be able to live and die more meaningfully.)

In this chapter, I am including several selections that I hope will help you see how confrontation with death and dying can enrich one's life and help one to become a more human and humane person. In the first selection, I share with you those events in my own personal life that I feel have been instrumental in molding my character and in leading me to choose this field of work. The second selection is a beautiful account by a physician of the experiences in his own life which set him apart from most doctors and made him a loving, feeling individual who is able to reach out to others, as a human being, leaving behind the "role" of doctor which restrains so many from doing what they feel is right and important. The third selection is the story of a young man's life and death written by a friend who cared enough to risk the pain of sharing his, emerging from the experience with cherished growth and understanding. The final piece of the chapter, a poem by a dying man to his wife, expresses the love they share that transcends physical life and death. This man, who through his illness began the organization "Make Today Count," is a symbol of the growth that can accompany the experience of dying for those who do not despair about how little time is left, but rather rejoice in what they have. Whether you are a professional working with dying patients, a dying patient yourself, or a loved one of a dying patient, I hope these selections will provide insights that you can apply to your own growth.

# Death as Part of My Own Personal Life

## Elisabeth Kübler-Ross, M.D.

*In the following pages, I would like to share with you some of the experiences of my life which I feel have contributed to making me what I am, which may have led me to the field of death and dying, and which have molded my views on death and life. You may find what I have to say interesting simply for these reasons. But more important, I believe, are the influences in my own personal life that coincide with and parallel threads weaving throughout all the selections in this book, from a variety of different sources. It is in these consistencies, between my life experiences and those of others, some of whom I have never met, that I think you may find some clues to the mysteries of life and death that may help guide you in your life.*

*To choose one example, I was fortunate as a child to have experienced death as a natural event, accepted with calm and lack of fear by the person dying. This, you may remember, was one of the factors found in the "Living until Death" study to predict good adjustment to dying. Like the priest to the Alaskan Indians, I have shared in a community's participation in the death and dying process, and I have personally felt the difference between that kind of familiar, comfortable environment as a setting for death and the sterile, impersonal atmosphere of a hospital. I have seen the ravages of war, and I have seen people emerge from it more understanding of the need for humanity in a too often inhumane world. Experiencing, rather than being shielded from, death, I have been able to understand it as an expected and integral part of life.*

*This work with dying patients has also helped me to find my own religious identity, to know that there is life after death and to know that we will be reborn again one day in order to complete the tasks we have not been able or willing to complete in this lifetime. It is in this context that I also begin to see the meaning of suffering and understand why even young children have to die.*

At the time of this writing I am a middle-aged physician who has

This essay was written especially for this volume. Used by permission of the author.

become well known throughout the country as "The Death and Dying Lady" (some less enthusiastic people may still occasionally refer to me as "The Vulture"). I spend a great deal of my life with terminal patients, dying children and adults, as well as their families. It may be of interest to take a look back, and try to determine what points and crossroads in my own life have made me go into such a peculiar specialty.

I was born on a warm summer day in Switzerland after a long and very wanted pregnancy. My parents had a six-year-old son and were very much looking forward to having a daughter. My mother was looking forward to making cute little dresses and to having someone with her when she did her fabulous baking and cooking, for which she was well-known.

The first impression both my parents had of me was of great dismay. I was barely two pounds, bald, and so tiny that I was clearly a disappointment. Little did anyone expect that this was only the beginning of more shocks; another two pound sister was born fifteen minutes later, followed by a six pound girl who finally met all the expectations of the new parents.

It is hard to say if my precarious introduction to life was the first "instigator" to going into this field. After all, I was not expected to live and if it had not been for the determination of my mother, I might not have survived. She strongly believed that such little infants could only survive if they received a great deal of tender loving care, frequent breast feedings, and the warmth and comfort that only home could give them—not the hospital. She cared for the three of us personally, nursed us every three hours, day and night, and it is said that she never slept in her bed for the first nine months. All three of us—needless to say—made it.

So perhaps the first significant lesson in my life was that it takes *one human being who really cares* to make a difference between life and death.

My next encounters with death were friendly ones. We grew up in a lovely village surrounded by farms. When my father's friend died (after a fall from a tree), we were part of the dying process and part of the grieving process. He lived long enough after the accident to call us into his bedroom to say goodbye to us. He also encouraged us to help his wife and children to save the farm. He was young, and in the midst of life, very rational and reasonable, and as much as I remember, there was no sign of fear.

I was a little girl at that time and my last visit with him filled me with great pride and joy. I am sure it was the fact that he called all of us children into his room personally and alone and had enough confidence in us to ask us for help for his beloved farm. I have never worked so hard in my life as during the next few summers and falls after his death—to bring in a good harvest. Each time we brought in a load of hay I was convinced that he could see us, and I saw his face shine with pride and joy.

When I was in second grade a new physician moved into our community. He was a quiet and rather withdrawn man, and since he came from another area little was known about him. His two little girls attended school with us. They were well behaved, pretty and rather sophisticated young ladies, and it took awhile until they became part of the village community, where outsiders were still viewed with a certain scepticism until they "proved themselves." The older of the two girls, about 10 years old at that time, became ill and the rumor spread fast that she had meningitis. Almost daily, worse news bulletins were passed in school and in the community house; one day she became blind, then paralyzed, and then she lost her hearing. Specialists came in from everywhere but to no avail. When she died the schools were closed, and more than half of the village attended her funeral. It started at her house, where the body was dressed in her favorite dress that she wore on her last day of school. Her family walked behind the hearse, followed by relatives and the teachers. All of us followed the long procession on foot until we reached the church where a brief and moving service was held. We then followed the family to the graveyard, where two men prepared the hole, and the casket was slowly put into the ground. All of us put a handful of soil on the casket. We sang a song and slowly moved away to leave the grieving family alone for a moment. Brigit was the first child who died in my life. She was not a personal friend, but all of us—the whole village—grieved with this family. We all shared the illness, the tragedy, the loss of her vision, her hearing—every aspect of the dying process with them—and we were able to accompany her on her last trip to the cemetery.

There was a feeling of solidarity, of common tragedy shared by a whole community. She was never removed from the village, or from her home. There was no impersonal hospital where she had to die in a strange environment. Everybody close to her was near her day and night.

How different this was from my own critical illness when I was about five years old. Suffering from pneumonia, I was taken to a children's hospital and kept in isolation for weeks. I was able to see my parents only through a glass window. Everything around me was strange, and as young as I was, I suffered most from lack of privacy. The isolation room was a glass cage, surrounded all around by glass walls. Baths were given in there and I spent most of my time dreaming about my "retreat in the hills", a little wild forest with a lot of underbrush where I would disappear to when someone at home upset me. I was longing for this quiet place where rabbits and birds, an occasional fox or harmless snake were my only companions. Being a triplet and too much in the limelight, a quiet retreat was essential to my own growth. Here in the hospital there was no escape. There was no familiar voice, touch, odor, not even a familiar toy. Everything was very clean and routine. There were no antibiotics at that time and no real treatment, thus little hope that I would survive. I could not talk to my parents when they came to visit me; I could only see their sad faces pressed towards the glass which separated me from the outside world. If it had not been for my vivid dreams and fantasies, I am sure I would not have survived this sterile place.

In my teens the war—with its destruction, bombs and refugees— broke out. Switzerland remained an island of peace, but we were reminded daily of the struggle for survival, the sacrifices of our neighbors, and the death toll outside our borders.

News slowly kept coming in about tortures of Jews and about the indescribable suffering of those who stood and spoke up; and finally, the stories of horrible concentration camps were confirmed.

My brother and father volunteered for the army and had posts along the German border. Innumerable families tried to swim across the river to reach the safety of Switzerland only to be machine gunned down by the Nazis. Many of them who made it left some members of their families behind, dead or doomed to die in work camps or gas chambers.

I made an oath that I would go and help these people as soon as it was possible to leave the country. In the meantime I spent my weekends in the hospital to volunteer and assist the thousands of refugees who escaped the Nazis. We de-loused hundreds of children, treated them for scabies and collected food, clothes, diapers and baby bottles. Months passed as fast as weeks. Then came the great day: PEACE. I spent it on the roof of the Kantonsspital, the largest hospital in Zurich. We carried every possible patient to the roof. It was virtually covered with wheelchairs and stretchers. Nobody complained; we wanted them to hear the bells—the bells of peace. Every single church—and there were over two hundred—rang at the exact same moment. Everybody cried, everybody held on to some-body. An old terminally ill woman said with a big happy smile on her face; "Now I can let go, now I can die. I wanted so badly to live long enough to see peace on earth come back."

Months later I hitchhiked through war-devastated Europe with a knapsack containing some essentials and a great deal of idealism and hope. I set out on a long journey, which took me through nine countries, working as a cook, a mason, a roofer, opening typhoid and first aid stations, crossing the Polish-Russian border with a Gypsy caravan, and last but most important perhaps, visiting Majdanek, one of the worst concentration camps where thousands of adults and children died in gas chambers or because of hunger, illness and torture. I can still see the barracks with little inscriptions of the victims, smell the odor of the crematoriums and see the wire mesh fence where few were able to crawl through only to be shot by the guards.

It was in this horrible place where I made the acquaintance of a young Jewish girl, herself a victim of the Nazis. She had been rescued from the concentration camp and dedicated herself to helping and rebuilding this war-devastated Europe.

It was hard for me to understand how a girl tortured almost to death was capable of helping the Germans who had killed almost her entire family. Through the months and years of suffering she had not grown bitter but became more and more aware of the need for more humanity in this world of inhumanity!

With people like her we made camp in Lucimia, at the river Wista in Poland. It was there that my plans to study medicine became a reality. It was there in the midst of suffering that I found my goal. It was there in the midst of poverty, isolation and suffering that I lived more than in all the years before or afterwards.

The three "lady doctors", as some referred to us, had worked long hours to take care of hundreds of patients who came from far away in search of hope, treatment, and perhaps some medicine. Our shelves were empty; we had nothing left. A small two room house served as the clinic. One room was used as a storage room. It contained a few chickens and eggs, butter and other foods that the patients brought as payment for our services. Up to fifty people worked in this camp, rebuilding one of the worst war-devastated places in Eastern Europe. They came and volunteered from many countries.

I was sleeping in a blanket under the sky when the weeping of a small child woke me. A mother sat silently next to me. She had walked three days and two nights to find our station, carrying a critically ill child in her arms. Janek was about three years old, hot and with glassy eyes, barely responding. He had typhoid, and there was nothing I could do for him. I brought the mother and child into the "clinic", offered them my blanket to lie down on the floor and to get some sleep. We had a cup of tea together in the middle of the night while I tried to convey to this woman that her long walk could not save her child.

She listened attentively and never took her eyes from me. When I finished what I had to say, she added very matter-of-factly: "You have to save this child; he is the last of my children who were all with me in the concentration camp." The fact that she and Janek survived was like a miracle. She sounded as if this made her only surviving son definitely immortal.

I have never felt so hopeless and helpless in my life. I would have done anything to save this boy. If she was anxious, she certainly did not show it. She sat calmly next to me sipping a cup of tea, waiting for further instructions. For a while I wondered how a woman could walk so many days carrying such a sick child in her arms. Then my thoughts wandered off to our empty medicine closet, to Janek, to the concentration camps . . . And before the night was over we were walking again; this time we headed toward L., where they had a hospital. We knew that the chances were slim. We also knew that they refused to take on any more patients. All the doctors, nurses and midwives had been killed by the Nazis, and the hospital was not only understaffed but overcrowded.

I remember vaguely reaching the stone walls which surrounded the place. I remember arguing with a Polish doctor that he had no heart, I appealed to his nationalism . . . I used every trick. He finally took Janek with the promise that we would not return until three weeks had passed. He would then either be buried or well enough to be taken home. The mother passed her child calmly into the physician's hands—there were no tears, no doubts, just a feeling of having accomplished a mission.

Mrs. W. became my new assistant. She kept a fire going to boil water for my syringes, she washed bandages and kept the clinic clean. She shared the blanket at night, and we worked together, speaking little. At night we would make a fire and all sit around it—singing. We would take a bath in the river and return to work. Patients came and left, days passed. One morning when I awoke my helper was gone. I missed her, but life was so full that I would have quickly forgotten her.

Some mornings later when I awoke I found a small white handkerchief next to my blanket. It was filled with earth. I presumed it was a superstitious sign of one of my patients and put it casually on the shelf. When night came and I cleaned up, I noticed this white handkerchief again. A villagewoman almost begged me to take notice of it. More to please her than for any other reason, I inspected this strange gift once more. It was regular dirt—but underneath the soil was a small piece of paper: "From Mrs. W. whose last of thirteen children you have saved, blessed Polish Earth."

Late that night I sat at the campfire, looking into the cloudless sky hoping that Mrs. W. would make it home safe and well. What a beautiful gift! Only a mother could have kept track of the time in this timeless environment. She knew that the time was right to pick up her son from the hospital. She took him home as she had always believed she would.

And because she lived—like hundreds of other families—in an earthhole—since all the houses were destroyed—she had nothing to give me. Nothing? She knew that I needed strength and faith to hold out for this work. So she simply took a handful of soil, walked another full day to the only remaining church and had the soil blessed to make it a special gift. She then slowly walked this endlessly long way through what we referred to as "Polish Siberia" back to our camp to quietly deliver her gift. Then, as quietly as she had come the first time, she slipped away during the night—to return to her son, the only child left of thirteen children!

I carried this soil with me and hung onto it when I was struck down in Germany on my way home. I kept it in the hospital in Germany where no one wanted to talk to me because they thought I was Polish. I hung onto it when I finally crossed the Swiss border—determined to return to a more settled "civilized" life in order to study medicine, to help more mothers and more terminally ill children—but hopefully with more tools, more medicines and more knowledge. The questions I ultimately wanted an answer for were: Where does a human being get the inner strength and equanimity to face such crises in life like this Polish mother? And more important perhaps: What turns people with the same human potential into beautiful, caring and loving, self-sacrificing human beings like that Jewish girl or instead into hateful, destructive creatures like the Nazis?

It is my deep hope that more people become concerned with these questions.

I am convinced that these experiences with the reality of death have enriched my life more than any other experiences I have had. Facing death means facing the ultimate question of the meaning of life. If we really want to live we must have the courage to recognize that life is ultimately very short, and that everything we do counts. When it is the evening of our life we will hopefully have a chance to look back and say: "It was worthwhile because I have really lived."

# Letter to Elisabeth: Dedicated to Carol

## Bal Mount, M.D.

*In the very moving piece that follows, a physician I know (who seems to me to be well equipped in both the science and art of medicine) shares with us the experiences he has had personally and professionally that make him different in my eyes–from the many who still cannot understand what we have to teach about the care of dying patients in our medical schools. On the way to the airport in Montreal, we had a personal conversation in which he seemed troubled and finally shared with me a sense of guilt which he became aware of during my lecture on the needs of the dying patient. He had been asked recently by a terminally ill student nurse for a consultation. He had looked at her pyelograms and X-rays but had "no time" to visit her personally. He was quite unaware of this behavior until he sat in my lecture, and it obviously troubled him. Before I said goodby to him, I asked him for two favors: First, to go and visit the patient on his way home in order to truly enjoy his weekend with his own family; and second, to write down for me some of the influences that have shaped his concept of death, distinguishing him from most of the physicians I have known since I began my work on death and dying. On the following pages is his response to me. I think you will find interesting parallels between his report of his life experiences with death and my own and other discussions of the subject in this book.*

My Dear Elisabeth,

Your fireside request that I put down on paper some of the influences that have shaped my concept of death gave me food for thought during the restless hours of last night. Forgotten experiences, not really forgotten, too indelible for that, merely dusty and stored away, were rediscovered, sorted, and examined.

---

"Letter to Elisabeth: Dedicated to Carol," by Bal Mount, M.D. This letter appears in print for the first time in this volume. Used by permission of the author.

I wandered into my father's small, book-lined library as my parents were studying a recent photograph. "My, how I've aged in the past three years", Dad commented in wonder. Mother agreed. I was six, but had it happened yesterday I could not recall more vividly the lump that swelled in my chest and the feeling of panic. Daddy is getting old. He will die soon.

Later the teacher asked me to stay behind after class, and, putting an arm around me tried to coax out an explanation for the silent tears that she had seen that afternoon. I couldn't bring myself to speak about my fears. Finally, in an all knowing tone she asked "Is there trouble at home?" Grateful for this means of escape I nodded, feeling somewhat guilty on noting her expression and sensing the deceptive appearance of domestic turmoil that I had thereby produced.

Two other childhood experiences surfaced last night when the dust was blown aside. The first also happened when I was six and concerned Miss S, a kindly milk and cookie giving spinster that lived close by. Miss S. was part of the family. She lived in a large home that had a subdued air to my young eyes. Now she was dying with metastatic cancer. On his last housecall before she died, Dad, in his wisdom, took me with him. He went in first, examined her and gave her the confidence of his calm assured presence and support.

A tall imposing man of uncompromising moral fiber, his approach to his dying patients had its origin in his deep concern for the suffering of others and his unfailing interest in their personal lives and feelings. Having asked Miss S if she would like to see me he led me to her bedside. Her gaunt jaundiced face, her smile of greeting, her thin outstretched hand, his ease in her presence, became fixed in my memory. For the first time I had looked into the face of death—a death that would be welcomed when it came as a passport to peace.

When I was fourteen my mother underwent surgery and, for a time during the postoperative period, her survival was in question. Vignette memories remain, my father's face etched with concern; his quiet careful words as he sat on my bed one night. "Your mother is really very sick"; our prayers that she would get better; moments spent in an empty hospital corridor outside the closed door to her room, attempting to imagine her in her sickness but being unable to; the thought that she might die. I was aware at a very early age of the transience of life.

Who could define the other events that coloured my early concept of death: the effects of a World War II conscious society, those radio programs listened to over a big brother's shoulder when mother was out. . . . "The Green Hornet". . . . "The Shadow". . . . "Inner Sanctum." And so into teenage years and the sunny fall Sunday afternoon when we took off to fly the 130 miles to visit my brother Jim away at medical school. We later were told that a connecting rod had broken. What we experienced was the head snapping vibrations of a wildly out of control bronco. We lost altitude quickly. Fences flashed past as we skimmed across ploughed fields. A haystack passed our wing tip. Cold perspiration, pounding pulses, black oil pouring over the fuselage, Dad's hand on my knee, "I am sorry, son, I guess this is it": the piledriver vibration of the straining engine—under high tension wires, across a country road into the line of stately elm trees, only to have the plane veer crazily as the right wing tore off on the asphalt. The Bonanza cartwheeled and jerked to a stop in front of a stone farm house. No one was seriously injured. A concept was reinforced—life is transient.

Medical school days: "Don't think I'm going to take time to teach, but you can come along if you like" thundered Ford Connell characteristically, his eyebrows arched emphatically, his head thrust forward so that his staring eyes were inches from my face. And so beloved "General Bullmoose", "Old Ironsides", our professor of medicine agreed to my tailing along on his weekly private Sunday morning medical rounds. A superb cardiologist and general physician, this great teacher could never resist the opportunity to demonstrate a clinical point, and thus started what was for me a series of career saving weekly immersions in general medicine. After two and a half hours of rounds, coffee and a doughnut together each week I would leave enriched. Standing in the hospital lobby the day we parted for the last time, one found that words of thanks merely ended up sticking in the throat and there was a flush that made you swallow hard. "Well Mount, you may not have learned much medicine but I hope you learned how to deal with people" he growled and turned on his heel as I caught a glimpse of the mirrored emotion in his brimming eyes. Maimonides said "Let me see in the sufferer the man alone". It was Ford Connell who perfected and lived out that great goal for generations of medical students at Queen's University.

I was still in the Recovery Room and coming out of the anaesthetic when my surgeon leaned down and confided, "It was a malignant tumor Bal". . . . When my mind cleared and I was back in my room there were no agonizing hours of doubt and fear. I already knew. "Why me?" Just out of medical school, wife pregnant—why me? But the thought was cut short. A few days earlier the assassination of

President Kennedy had stunned the world. In the words of Sir Alec Douglas Home, Prime Minister of England, it was "One of those times in life when heart and mind stand still. Everything in one cried out in protest." And we had all asked why couldn't it have been me and not him? No; with that thought in mind, one could hardly ask "why me?"

But as the days passed an uneasiness was added to the weighty concern of the malignancy. Why did my family not seem to be more greatly concerned? Oh they were concerned, of course they were. And yet they seemed so cheery and ready to discuss things that seemed so damned unimportant. And the irony. As close as we were, a medical family, we couldn't discuss our fears. The only direct references to the tumor were my brother's welcome humorous quips post surgery about having a brother who had been filleted and Dad's comment on the pathology report. It was only much later that I was able to tear down "the conspiracy of silence" and hear for the first time of the tearful confrontations between parents and wife . . . the concern, the love.

Any re-creation of those bleak days would be incomplete without noting the pivotal point that personal faith played. The prayers of friends, family, and myself brought clearer realization regarding what to pray for—not for cure, but for understanding, calm, and strength. I was amazed to find that resources were there and a vital new awareness of what personalized faith meant. Resources appeared during the darkest hours of despair.

When my in-laws gave me the volume containing Tom Dooley's three books a year earlier, they had inscribed in it "Hoping you'll find fulfillment as he did". . . . These wishes now seemed to have taken an unexpected short cut to reality. . . . I grinned at the grim twist of fate but then began to read the volume that I previously had been too busy to read. The grace of that young Irish American surgeon and saint who started the medical aid program to Southeast Asia, as he faced his own terminal malignancy, was impressive.

Through Tom Dooley, two real options became vividly real. The answer to "How much time do I have?" became "There are "x" days left and, however long "x" is, there are only two possibilities, to live them in despair or to really live them to the hilt, making them count, as Dooley did." The choice was clear and a great weight was lifted from my shoulders. It would be impossible to exaggerate the significance of that moment. It led to the next realization, that really we're all in the same boat, with "x" days to live. Even if cured of the cancer, I'm a day closer to dying today than yesterday. We all are. For all of us then, it isn't the quantity of life but the quality that counts. It took a malignancy to put life into perspective and to open for me the concept of dying as a growing experience.

I was years later to stand in rapt fascination at the back of a packed auditorium and listen to you describe the series of steps we may pass through in reaching a point of acceptance of our terminal state. But if my illness was my personal introduction to the truths I was later to hear about acceptance by the patient; then an event a few months later introduced us as a family to the feelings of the bereaved. Three months after my tumor my brother's wife died during childbirth. A brilliant pianist and devoted wife and mother, Betty was a vibrant focal point of our family. She was twenty-eight years old. The anger, guilt, denial-rejection (to the point of physically vomiting) were overwhelming.

A final hard lesson was waiting lest one presume proficiency in facing death on the basis of previous experience. In a vivid flashback I see my six year old's expression change from one of wild excitement to one of fear as he fought to control his hurtling bicycle. He had raced down the forbidden hill to a point opposite me when the wheel turned and he plummeted over the handlebars driving his face into the cement. He was deeply unconscious and decerebrating as I turned him over in horror and disbelief. In the minutes and days that followed I cursed God from the depths of my being. My son recovered but I never again presumed to have mastered the "acceptance of death question." Like the arms of Don Quixote's windmill we must face death anew, each time it presents itself.

It was ten years later. I walked into the patient's room and introduced myself. "I'm glad to see you," she stated, "I've been expecting you for several days." Carol looked wanly from her stacked pillows and forced a thin smile. I took the opportunity to both explain my tardiness and open the path to frank discussion with this young patient, a student nurse. "I'm sorry I was delayed. Does the name Elisabeth Kübler-Ross mean anything to you?"

"Yes, I heard her speak a year and a half ago when she was in Montreal. She has taken all the fear out of dying" . . . . . And your statement, Elisabeth, that the "best teachers are the dying patients themselves," jolted into new meaningfulness. Lesson one from Carol just completed, "never postpone anything you plan to do with or to a dying person." For three days I had had her consultation on my mind. Just not enough time. . . . "Twenty year old white female; metastatic ovarian carcinoma, hypertension, hypercalcuria, seizures, non-visualization of her left kidney on pyelography and poor visualization of the right kidney." Was there anything to be done urologically?

I had meant to see her immediately. You were coming to town. Perhaps this student nurse had heard of you; you could get together—a potential mountain top experience for Carol. But I had to sound her out first. I could hardly wander in with Elisabeth Kübler-Ross without finding out if she knew she was terminally ill. There just wasn't time. Irony again. I did have time to see her pyelogram and assess the medical problem that I knew was beyond help, but there wasn't time to assess her emotional needs—the only area we might have helped. Mountain top missed. I had just left you at the airport. Air Canada flight to Chicago; and the words "She has taken all the fear out of dying" made me feel sick.

It seemed to Carol that an eternity had passed but it had been only eight weeks since her sister's wedding. There had been a month of nagging abdominal aches before that and three hospitalizations, blood drawn, X-rays, ECG's, EEG's, and surgery since. "Undifferentiated anaplastic carcinoma". When you're twenty how should you feel? "Who or what helped you the most, Carol?" "One of the residents. He took the time one morning after the entourage had left, to wait and comment, 'Hey, I hear you didn't sleep well last night. How come?' So we talked and I felt so much better." Lesson two from Carol: "it takes so little effort to make such a big difference."

On my second visit to Carol, her parents were present. One sensed a degree of tension as the weather, her friends, the flowers, her radio were discussed in succession. In the hall her father confided that it was tough and that he had had to leave the room on several occasions to avoid breaking down. And together we discussed the alternatives. "I don't think she really knows the situation," he said dubiously. Earlier the same day Carol had squeezed my hand urgently and asked "Do you think there is a life after death?" With a tear welling in her eye and a smile that was wistful yet impish she added "I sure hope so. I'm not afraid of dying, but I'm afraid of hurting my family and my boyfriend. I don't want them to suffer." The need for frank discussion was evident. Carol's father returned to the room and took her hand. In the flood of openness that followed, the conspiracy of silence was broken.

To the end Carol demonstrated her courage, spirit, and strength. Her acceptance, so real on one level, was accompanied by a shield of denial—hope which she needed to hide behind less and less as the days passed, until the point with her father and me beside her, when she commented looking up at her father and holding tightly to our hands, "This can't go on. I want to die. I'm sorry to say that, Daddy, and I love you so much . . ." In her final days Carol was a patient teacher as we awkwardly learned of our deficiencies as a hospital ministering to the terminally ill. The nurse who thought that doctors were not supposed to be left alone with Carol because they might say something to upset her; the clergyman who attended her at the end but couldn't speak to her needs because he didn't know where she was along the road to faith; the doctors who arranged for her second EEG that week, on her last day alive: all learned from Carol.

A year and a half earlier, in a packed McGill auditorium two of us shared an evening with you. For me it was an evening of fresh insights as I understood the pathway I had travelled with a malignancy, in a fresh light. For Carol it was a spark that led her to write her term paper on "The Child's View of Death." How little we suspected that evening how short a time it would be before the pupil became the teacher, and on that last day the three of us crossed paths again. Your letter to Carol arrived the day before she died. As I left the hospital that night it seemed to me that we had a long way to go and that there was a better way than the present one to meet the needs of the terminally ill. Carol had shown us our strengths but more often, our obvious deficiencies. She reminds us as we review our attitudes towards the dying that "we have promises to keep and miles to go before we sleep." *

Note: Dr. Bal Mount and a caring crew are now working on a special PCU (Palliative Care Unit) at the Royal Victoria Hospital in Montreal where all the needs of the terminally ill patient are met, a unit that is also a fulfilment of one of my dreams.

E. K. R.

---

* Robert Frost, "Stopping by the Woods on a Snowy Evening."

# Louie

## Shirley Holzer Jeffrey

*I have said earlier that it is the quality of life that counts and not the number of years we live. Carol is an example of this as she has touched many lives in her short span of life. Louie is another example. Louie had a difficult life and finally found acceptance and love, only to surrender all this to the grim reaper death. A brief story of his life and death is written and published in his memory and in tribute to this beautiful, young couple, Louie and Diane, whose love will touch others and who may help to make you more aware of the need to live and to love and to allow yourself to grow **today**—so that you may express, one day, the same gratitude for life that has been.*

LOUIE: Tall, slender, sixteen. He had lived in at least seven different homes, and had no one but an elderly grandmother, who cared enough about him to stand by him and help him to grow into the person he had the potential to be. And the old grandmother was becoming senile, and lived in a nursing home. The seven homes where he had lived had each decided, for one reason or another, that the nurturing of a young boy into manhood was more than they cared to undertake.

That was when he entered our lives. He had been living at the YMCA while attending school at our local high school. He came to live with us—a shy, sensitive boy, afraid to trust people, and struggling hard to know who he was. He was a pleasant boy who tried hard to convince himself that there were positive things in his experience. He emphasized what he had learned about people by living in many homes. He protected himself from the anger of so many rejections by building walls of rationalization which allowed him to cope with his

---

experience. But buried deep inside there had to be much anger and hurt. People could not be trusted because they had let him down too many times.

As Louie sought the answer to the question, "Who am I?", he was unable to point to a family of flesh and blood. He treasured the pictures and articles about the family from which he came. His parents were both dead by the time he was five. The mementos were little help to a teenage boy seeking his identity. He chose to find identity with his peers in the only way he knew. He became the best dressed boy in the school. In clothes he found recognition. He wanted to be judged to be "college", which was the expression of the day used to describe someone noticed and admired by his peers. He bought a sports car and with it gained mobility and recognition. He sensed dimly that security did not really rest in these things. But his experience had taught him well that it did not rest in relationships with people either. In late night talks we often were able to penetrate the wall a little and witness our own deep concern for his being.

Louie chose to go on to college, and in that choice he opened a door to many new struggles. The vacation conversations revealed the depth of the struggle that was his. He dated a warm and outgoing girl who attracted him because she obviously cared about him and she reminded him of the one adult woman in his background whom he admired. She was attracted to him partly because of his background. He was different. She wanted to make up for what he had missed. After college they married, but she was not prepared for the walls of protection that he had maintained. In marriage those walls that had protected him so long were being threatened and he had to agonize over the desire to be close and yet the great fear that risking trust produced. "If I trust her she may let me down too. How can I be sure I won't be hurt again? Do I dare to trust?"

That struggle was great enough for one life. But then he became ill. He went to the Mayo Clinic, where after a number of tests the doctor came into his room and announced: "Well, we know what is wrong now: you have Hodgkin's Disease." With that the doctor turned on his heels and left Louie and his wife, Diane, in the wake of shock. Horror swept over them. There were a thousand thoughts, and many many questions that beat upon their beings. The questions needed answers: What is involved in Hodgkin's? What does the future hold? What are the chances for survival? How long? What will be done? What kind of treatment is there? Is there any hope? These questions a doctor could face with them. Instead the two young people sat in that hospital room away from home and friends, and faced a vast and dark unknown in utter agony. And there was no one there who would take time to listen to their hurt, to their questions, to their anguish. There was no one.

The chaplain stopped in. He might have provided a listening ear to hear the feelings that were being encountered. Instead he engaged in inane chatter and superficial talk about their home town. When he walked through that door to the hospital room he had an opportunity to minister. By the time he had set the tone for informal chatter, the two young people wanted only to get rid of him. His hollow words rang as clashing cymbals in the closed and tight room of their agony.

Louie and Diane came home from the clinic with the knowledge that Louie's disease had already progressed far. Hope was at best very thin. What does the future hold? What is going to happen? Why do others grow old while life for him will be short at best? Hodgkin's Disease!!! What is it going to mean? The greatest fears burn through the body like great electric shocks. "I'm going to die. I'll lose my good looks. My hair will fall out. I'll get puffy. I'll become unattractive. How will Diane take it? She married me because I was strong and she wanted a normal life with home and children. I won't be able to give her that. It makes me feel guilty and angry and helpless. She married a good looking, healthy young man, with dreams of home and family, and she is stuck with an ugly, sick creature, who will get sicker and who can give her nothing. Every time I see an old person I hate them just because they are alive." Such feelings gave rise to much hostility, and anger, and self rejection, and self indulgence. Coupled with the loss of his image as a strong man came the loss of hope to be a success. "I'm not going to live long enough to prove to all those who didn't believe in me, that I can be a success." Despair, frustration, anger, fear, and terror became daily companions.

Notes of concern began to come. Louie discovered that people did care about him, and hurt because he was hurting. There were those who said, "It's so hard to understand why God lets such a thing happen." They made Louie feel guilty and intensified the natural question, "Why me?" Someone said, "God does not will for you to be sick, but he does will for you to grow in the experience that is yours." Others told of people they knew and tragedies with which they were familiar in hope that another person's misfortune would ease Louie's hurt. Such stories only made Louie feel that the person did not want to identify with his hurt and feel with him. One person wrote, "Thinking of you in faith, hope and love." That note was much appreciated. It communicated that someone cared and hurt and hoped. That is what

Louie needed to know. No one could erase his situation, but people could offer him the support of their caring. Someone sent him the words of the Twenty-second Psalm. That psalmist captured utterly much of the feeling that Louie and Diane were experiencing.

The Christmas season came and Louie was worse. He had to be hospitalized. He was frightened and felt so alone and vulnerable. The cards began to come; flowers arrived; and then someone from work brought a hundred dollars collected from fellow workers to help with expenses. Louie was amazed and moved to tears. He couldn't believe that people could care so much about him. He had built his life on the foundation that people did not care. After the hospitalization he said one day, "One good thing about Hodgkin's, if there can be a good thing, I've found out that people really do care about me. It's hard for me to handle, but I am glad."

In the first months he struggled with a question that he would have to deal with over and over. "If I'm not going to live long, why shouldn't I do anything at all that I want to do?" It hooked itself into specifics at different times: "Why should I work?", "Why shouldn't I eat steak every night?" "Why shouldn't I buy anything I want?" "Why shouldn't I stay high on drugs if I want?" Louie had to discover for himself that neither escape nor indulgence give life meaning.

Louie did become puffy as he had feared, but he did not lose his hair. The daily agony of living with the knowledge of the disease made him fantasize that he would meet a girl who had Hodgkin's and they would go off to an island somewhere together. This fantasy described the deep longing for someone who would really understand his feelings, and that person would know them only if she had actually experienced them.

A year passed. Another Christmas came. And Louie found himself in the hospital again. This time he learned that the disease had progressed, and that the drug that they had been using no longer worked. His lungs were bad and his backbone was near breaking. They would have to give large doses of cobalt to strengthen the weak spot. A new drug would be used and it would not be as comprehensive as the other, but neither would it produce the terrible nausea. The news brought about a new wave of terror. After two weeks he completed the cobalt treatment and went home only to return within seventy-two hours nearly dead. His condition was critical. He responded to no one. And we had to deal with the prospect of losing him. At four in the afternoon he opened his eyes and said the first words of the day. We were relieved. He would make it this time.

Platelets poured into his bloodstream had brought Louie back with great rapidity. One day he was nearly dead, and the next he was up shaving. He was confronted with how rapidly he could change—both directions.

We talked. He said he was glad to be in the hospital because then people realized how sick he is, and that his condition is serious. "I don't have to pretend to be strong when I am in the hospital. People come to see me and they know that I am really sick." There was another side of him, though, that feared being weak. "I can't accept being weak. I'm so angry. And I don't know what to do. I cry over every little thing. I can't control my emotions." He was so frustrated and frightened. He later said, "The thought of what is going on inside my body is terrifying. I can get so much worse and not even know it. Before I checked my nodes every morning. Now I'll have to check the bones too????" The unknown is an awful monster to encounter.

In the weeks following this last hospitalization Louie felt that death was around the corner and he became terrified. The only way he knew how to cope was to take sleeping pills and other drugs in such quantity as to knock himself out. He nearly succeeded in knocking himself out permanently and thus had to return to the hospital.

The terror itself frightened him. He hated it. "Why can't I be like the man who didn't tell anyone that he had cancer? Wasn't he a much more noble person than I am?" I told him, "Perhaps the man was even more terrified. If no one knew, then he could pretend he wasn't sick and didn't have to admit it even to himself." A look of relief ran across Louie's face. He went on, "When I went down for a liver scan there was a man crying out, "Why can't you stop all this and let me die?" I said, "You are worrying about what it will be like." He told me how scared he was. And finally he told of reading of the football player with Hodgkin's who was going to the Mardi Gras, but died before he got there. The future is so unknown. When will death come? Will there be warning? Will it be gradual or fast? Can it be avoided? The fears came tumbling out.

I went home and wrote to Louie:

> I do not know
> If you feel it
> As I feel it.
> Maybe not.
> But for me
> There is a dimension

Of love
That I have for you
That is absolutely
Unique!!
I know for sure
That with each passing
Month you become
More precious to me.
And one of the reasons
This is so,
Is because you do not
Hide behind a mask,
But share
Your hurts and sorrows,
Worries and dreams,
Fantasies and pleasures,
Anger and insights.
Your struggles shared
Have brought a dimension
To my being
That was not there before.
And I thank you for sharing with me.
I hurt with you just a tiny bit of your hurt.
And even that tiny bit
Is sometimes hard for me to handle.

There is no doubt that I feel weak
As do you.
And I say "Praise God for weakness felt."
For somehow or other
In weakness feelings shared
There is a meaning never experienced
By the so called strong,
Who need to deny their weakness feelings.

Louie framed the tribute and hung it on his bedroom wall. Its assurance had meaning for him. Too often feelings do not get verbalized. The permanence of the written word is often treasured by the recipient.

Louie has died. His fears of a lingering death were unnecessary. His agony was but a week. But in that week there was so much physical pain and so much frustration. What he had feared for two years had come to pass. There was the agony to be endured. Perhaps it is as necessary for growth of the spirit as is heat for the tempering of steel. The agony was followed by the great affirmation three hours before he died. For one entire half hour he communicated with all the tones of the conquering spirit. There were no words, just a continuous and intense, "Ummmmmm Hummmmmm, um hum, ummmmm hummmmmm!!!!!!" What did it mean? Surely it involved gratitude; gratitude for what had been, but also for what was to be. As his spirit remained with us it seemed to take on a bit of the eternal. There was such strong and intense tone. It was hard to believe that enough strength could be summoned for such a witness. UMMMMMMM HUMMMMMM!!!!!!! ummm hummm! HUMMMMMMM HUMMMMMMMM!!!!!!!!!!

Death, it is no longer just a word I wish to avoid. It is an experience the near side of which I felt as I sat by and hurt and agonized as Louie was engaged in the act of dying. Early in the week I felt the pain, the frustration, the fear and the anxiety. He said he would wait to talk about it until Friday. Later in the week I felt the courage, the confrontation, the agony and the frustration. I was afraid. I wanted to escape. I wanted to be free.

On Friday I felt the conquest, the conquering, and finally the anticipation. I felt my soul bared as it had never been before. Surely those were by far the most emotion filled moments of my entire life. His eyes were wide, he held Diane's hand with great strength and uttered his song of affirmation: Ummmm Hummmm! Ummmmmm hummmmm!! Ummmmmm Hummmmm!!!!!!! And before my very eyes I saw that dying is a birth. It is terribly, terribly hard. It may be the hardest thing a person ever does. But one does emerge from the dark into the light.

Louie's conquering spirit bore witness to a new chapter about which we have only been given a hint.

I shall be richer all my life for this sorrow! New insights about life have been born. Life is to be lived by striking a line through every minus and turning it into a plus. If agony must be experienced, there are those who are ready to bear some of the burden. Where there is suffering the gift of courage is given. Courage comes from without as well as from within. The important moments in life are those shared with others, whatever the cost may be: When hurts are shared, closeness is born. The gift of love is a most precious gift, and it is possible to express it most fully at the end of earthly life. I shall be richer all my life for this sorrow. New insights about death have emerged. Death is another beginning, not an end. Death is but a new birth into a new state. Death is not to be feared, any more than is birth. When the body ceases to be, the spirit emerges, free and unencumbered. I shall be richer all my life for this sorrow!

> Sorrow:
> It hurts deep down inside.
> One feels diminished,
> Less than he has been.
> Empty,
> Bereft—
> Forlorn and incomplete.
> Sorrow is a painful word
> But if someone is there
> To share the feeling
> It becomes endurable
> And in the scheme of things
> A time of being
> That includes great emotion
> And thus a time of closeness,
> Growing and becoming someone more
> Than we have been before.

### IN MEMORIAM

> We sprinkle the ashes—
> All that tangibly remains
> Of Louis Peter Knudsen.
> But thank God for the intangibles—
> The impact of his life on ours.
> We remember:
>     —the smile
>     —the frown
>     —the quizzical look
>     —the love
>     —the courage
>     —the hurt
>     —the sorrow
>     —the significant moments
>     —the fun times
>     —the searching times
>     —the moments of risk
>     —the great time of affirmation
> As long as we live

We will bear the imprint
Of that influence.
He opened many doors for us—
Doors to whole new sets of meanings.
We will forever be sensitized
As to the importance of life.
Because of Louie we will live differently.


## LOVE—GRATITUDE

The agony is so great . . .
And yet I will stand it.
Had I not loved so very much
I would not hurt so much.
But goodness knows I would not
Want to diminish that precious love
By one fraction of an ounce.
I will hurt,
And I will be grateful to the hurt
For it bares witness to
The depth of our meanings,
And for that I will be
Eternally grateful.

# For My Wife, Wanda: Love Will Never Go Away

## Orville Kelly

*Looking back over this manuscript I am thinking of the many people—friends and patients— I have lost over the past few years. Ernest Becker, the author of "The Denial of Death" died a few weeks after I was privileged to review his manuscript. He finished a true masterpiece a few weeks before he died. Jacques Choron, another admired author, died just as I completed his manuscript on "Suicide", and Alsop followed a few months ago. Carol, Louie, and many others left their imprint. One terminally ill patient who makes a nationwide imprint is Orville Kelly—a man in his forties, full of cancer, who through his suffering has started an organization "Make Today Count" People of all ages with terminal illnesses are getting united with the sole purpose of combating the loneliness and isolation of the terminally ill, to share and help each other. Naturally Orville Kelly will long be remembered as the initiator of this nationwide organization. But what we should not ever forget is that—behind all this work—all these creative, innovative ideas born out of suffering and despair—is the dying man who would love to live and who knows he has to bid adieu to his loved ones.*

*Orville's own feelings and consolation come through in his own poem given to me as a gift I will always treasure:*

> Spring, and the land lies fresh green
> Beneath a yellow sun.
> We walked the land together, you and I
> And never knew what future days would bring.
> Will you often think of me,
> When flowers burst forth each year?
> When the earth begins to grow again?
> Some say death is so final,

But my love for you can never die.
Just as the sun once warmed our hearts,
Let this love touch you some night,
When I am gone,
And loneliness comes—
Before the dawn begins to scatter
Your dreams away.

Summer, and I never knew a bird
Could sing so sweet and clear,
Until they told me I must leave you
For a while.
I never knew the sky could be so deep a blue,
Until I knew I could not grow old with you
But better to be loved by you,
Than to have lived a million summers,
And never known your love.
Together, let us, you and I
Remember the days and nights,
For eternity.

Fall, and the earth begins to die,
And leaves turn golden-brown upon the trees.
Remember me, too, in autumn, for I will walk with you,
As of old, along a city sidewalk at evening-time,
Though I cannot hold you by the hand.

Winter, and perhaps someday there may be
Another fireplace, another room,
With crackling fire and fragrant smoke,
And turning, suddenly, we will be together,
And I will hear your laughter and touch your face,
And hold you close to me again.
But, until then, if loneliness should seek you out,
Some winter night, when snow is falling down,
Remember, though death has come to me,
Love will never go away!

# 6
# Death: The Final Stage of Growth

We end this book by coming full circle, back to the title and theme of the book—death as the final stage of growth. We have looked at death and dying from a number of angles to open up your perspective on the issue. We have tried to show you death as a meaningful, growth-inducing aspect of life, to get you to think about how the study and experience of death can help enrich and give meaning to your existence on this earth. Selections have been chosen to help communicate this message as well as explain the necessity of facing death in order to understand and accept it as an integral part of life.

I can think of no better selection to end this book on death and growth than one called "Dying as the Last Stage of Growth." The important message here, beyond its integration and reiteration of the ideas already discussed, is that dying is something we human beings do continuously, not just at the end of our physical lives on this earth. The stages of dying that I have described apply equally to any significant change (e.g., retirement, moving to a new city, changing jobs, divorce) in a person's life, and change is a regular occurrence in human existence. If you can face and understand your ultimate death, perhaps you can learn to face and deal productively with each change that presents itself in your life. Through a willingness to risk the unknown, to venture forth into unfamiliar territory, you can undertake the search for your own self—the ultimate goal of growth. Through reaching out and committing yourself to dialogue with fellow human beings, you can begin to transcend your individual existence, becoming at one with yourself *and* others. And through a lifetime of such commitment, you can face your final end with peace and joy, knowing that you have lived your life well.

# Dying as the Last Stage of Growth

## Mwalimu Imara

*In this piece, the author pulls together many of the ideas touched upon in earlier parts of the book. He explains that we must learn to die in order that we may learn to live, that growing to be who you truly are requires sometimes that you die to the life chosen for you by society, that each new step of growth involves a throwing off of more of the shackles restraining you. He shows that in order to grow, you must continuously die and be reborn, much as a caterpillar becomes a butterfly. And he stresses that although you receive your final opportunity for growth when you are standing at death's doorstep, your growth should not wait for this crisis in your life. By understanding the growth-producing properties of dying, you can learn to "die" and grow at any point you choose. Finally, he explains the qualities that predict your being able to deal comfortably and productively with death. These are the same qualities that distinguish a growing human being at any stage in his or her life.*

> Health is not equivalent to happiness, surfeit, or
> success. It is foremost a matter of being wholly one
> with whatever circumstances we find ourselves in.
> Even our death is a healthy event if we fully
> embrace the fact of our dying. . . . The issue is
> awareness, of living in the present. Whatever our
> present existence consists of, if we are at one with
> it, we are healthy.
> (Latner, p. 64)

My life at this moment seems to be one long line of growth experiences. At one place, one way of living became something I could no longer envision myself as being a part of, something that put me out of phase with what I felt myself to be. I died to those situations and

---

went through the agony and rebirth in a new city, a new country, a new job, and a new trade. When being a printer no longer felt right to me, the old nagging call to the ministry became stronger, I pulled up from my job, my business connections, my expensive tastes, and went to college for seven years to learn about the life-style of ministry. At thirty-one I was giving up the safety and comfort of a life as a successful businessman for the god-knows-what of the world of the religious professional. I remember eleven years earlier having left the relatively liberal atmosphere of Montreal for the racially restrictive climate of the United States. I wanted to leave my hometown for some strange place, why, I don't know. I did know that home had become too much of something that was not me. So, in fear and trembling, I left Canada for the brimstone and hellfire of New York.

Take a look at your life. What were those moments of chosen separation and pain when you were about the business of your own growth, when all the hounds of heaven could not have stayed you from those acts of your becoming. We may seek new professions or new locations or simply begin to experience ourselves as new in a therapeutic situation—whatever the situation, our experience of our own growth is really filled with anxiety and fraught with a sense of danger, as it is with excitement and fulfillment, as it is with pain as well as joy. Human life, my life and your life, have potential for this growth experience from the first moment at birth until our last breath at death.

We may be healthy persons with few major conflicts and splits in our sense of self, but our being spiritually-psychically sound humans does not eliminate the inevitable crises and fears that accompany growth and change. When we abandon the old familiar patterns of life, whether voluntarily or involuntarily, we always have a sense of risk-taking. When the new situation involves changes which may have grave consequences for our future well-being, the level of anxiety is bound to be great. Abandoning old ways and breaking old patterns is like dying, at least dying to old ways of life for an unknown new life of meaning and relationships. But living without change is not living at all, not growing at all. Dying is a precondition for living. Growth is a precondition for living. To limit the process is to exist as compressed beings.

In all of our growth situations except one, we can look forward to new vistas, new goals, new projects, and new enriching relationships. When we look forward to that time of dreaded news when our own death becomes imminent reality, we draw back in fear and rejection.

That is the one journey, the one labor few of us look forward to. Fear of that final separation, death, is natural. The thought of sleep without dreams, timelessness without concern and conversation with others is the most difficult thing we humans face.

Where there is love there is the anxiety about loss of life, and love it is that makes the loss of life in the psychical sense a dreaded thing, because death appears as the end of love, which is life.

(Haroutunian, p. 89)

We abhor and reject the moment when we will confront the nearness of our death. But the dying stage of our life can be experienced as the most profound growth event of our total life's experience. The shock, the pain and the anxiety are great, but if we are fortunate enough to have time to live and experience our own process, our arrival at a plateau of creative acceptance will be worth it.

Death is not a shock to our systems when we read about it in a book or discuss it philosophically in an armchair. The feelings of powerlessness and isolation come from our whole being and not our intellectual fantasies. The problem of death, in general, does not reach us in the core of our being. Only when it is "my" imminent death or the imminent death of someone I love do I feel the pangs of "life-hunger". The soul in torment is a person tortured from attachment to life, a torture which surges through our whole being, chilling us to our heart one minute and breaking us out in a flushing sweat the next. This is our frantic struggle to clutch at life while slipping over the brink to death. This is the self in battle with the non-self. The concrete possibility of our own imminent death is so great a shock that our first response must be denial. Thomas Bell, the author of IN THE MIDST OF LIFE, an autobiographical account of his own struggle with his own terminal situation, wrote:

Now and then the whole thing becomes unreal. Out of the middle of the night's darkness, or bringing me to a sudden, chilling halt during the day, the thought comes: This can't be happening to me. Not to me. *Me* with a malignant tumor? *Me* with only a few months to live? Nonsense. And I stare up at the darkness, or out at the sunlit street, and try to encompass it, to feel it. But it stays unreal.
Perhaps the difficulty is my half-conscious presumption that such things happen, should happen, only to other people. . . . People who are strangers, who really don't mind, who . . . are born solely to fill such quotas. Whereas I am me. Not a stranger. Not other people. Me!

I can see how you might have some difficulty in reading about his experience or seeing a person you know and love go through a similar experience, and still consider this pain and anguish to be the beginning of a potential growth experience. But it is just that. The pain is great because the loss is great. Death separates us from all that we hold dear, including our very selves. It is the ultimate of separations. And unlike other growth situations, we have little choice as to whether or not the separation will occur. However, what is in our control is the quality of the separation experience—making it "life" affirming or life-denying.

When the things we value most in life are destroyed, we can respond in several ways. We can live a life of depressed feelings and in extreme circumstances, give up investing in life entirely by developing a life of psychotic separation. This is the ultimate or extreme despair. The second alternative is to conceal the negative of our existence from consciousness. This is always an attempt at concealment because the defense is seldom effective for very long especially in situations of extreme stress like those involving our own death or the death of a significant other. The third alternative, I call religious. It is investing ourselves in creative and appreciative relationships with others. Becoming open to other people and remaining open to them is more easily said than done in time of crisis. It is especially difficult if we have not been in the practice of relating that way with others. In those moments when we experience the pain of our own dying and the dying of others, we are not likely to reach out to give or receive comfort or support unless our lives have been previously open to others in situations of joy, sorrow, anger and hate. This third response, our reaching out to others, is the step leading to a growth experience for the terminally ill person.

Our struggle for growth as we approach death is "the struggle . . . for meaning and significance of our person." Being, existing at this time of crisis *"is to mean something to someone else."* As we mature as adults, the threat of losing relationships with other significant persons in our lives is greater than the fear of losing our own life. We are animals who think of ourselves through our transactions with other persons. We are basically social being fellowpersons. And we cannot break our bonds with one another without becoming of no value. Since our highest values focus on ourselves in relation to others, death means termination of transaction with others or a "failure in communion". (Haroutunian, p. 83)

## A CASE STUDY

Several years ago when I was a student chaplain, there was an old lady who taught me what growth during the final stages of life really meant. We were seated in the interviewing room with Miss Martin. It was our regular Wednesday morning Death and Dying seminar conducted by Dr. Elisabeth Kübler-Ross. Miss Martin was one of our patients, who was willing to attend the seminar and talk to us about what her experience as a terminal patient was like. Miss Martin, Dr. Ross, and I sat facing one another, our chairs and the patient's wheelchair forming an intimate triangle in the small room. The students and staff were sitting in the observation room beyond the glass partition.

Miss Martin looked serene and soft in her blue nightgown. Her quiet voice, so different in tone from its loud stridency of months past, raised thoughtfully the regrets and pains of her past and her present to share with us and the students beyond the partition. We listened to the hardships and loneliness facing a single woman making her own way in the man's domain of business during the 1930s. We listened to her recount and recall the steps by which she became so alienated from her brother and sister, that even now when cancer was consuming her intestines, they would not travel a few hundred miles to visit her on her deathbed. Quietly she continued to speak.

Her voice trailed to a stop. Her head tilted a little to one side and her eyes seemed to focus on some vision, some thought far into the deep recesses of her being. Then she looked up at the glass screen separating her from the crowd in the other room and she said with a quiet firmness:

I have lived more in the past three months than I have during my whole life. . . . I wish I knew forty years ago what I know now about living. I have friends. Thank you.

We cried. All of us. Nurses, social workers, ministers, physicians, all crying for that miracle that was Miss Martin. Here, before us was a woman, an old woman, who had lived a long life with few friends and close relationships of any kind. Here was a woman with tremendous will and presence who could still frighten people who crossed her. She had grown bitter in her ruthless encounter with the world of her experience, taking but unable to give or receive from anyone, that is, until she met us. The miracle of Miss Martin was the transformation from a life-style of hardness to the open softness of the beautiful old woman before us at the seminar. The growth of Miss Martin was no sudden conversion. It was a long, almost daily battle lasting several months. Many of the staff bore the psychic scars to prove it.

You should have met that sweet old lady several months before the seminar. She became one of my hospital "Parishioners" as the result of an urgent request for a chaplain from the charge day nurse of her unit. I stopped by the nursing station on my way to the patient's room to see if there was anything I should know. The charge nurse on the unit, usually a kind, considerate person, was not in any such mood that day as she gave me the scoop on Miss Martin, the unit's number one problem. It was the first time that I had heard any patient referred to with such colorful, yet unprintable, epithets. From my encounter later that day, I would have to agree with all the epithets.

I was told that the patient, Miss Martin, was recovering from rather extensive abdominal surgery for cancer, and the more she healed, the more demanding, abusive, foul-mouthed, and cantankerous she became. The chaplain's office was called in as a last ditch effort to sweeten her up a little for the staff's sake until she was well enough to be sent to a nursing home.

Reluctantly, I went to meet Miss Martin. She was everything the nurse had promised, in triplicate. She was, indeed, a very graceless old lady. My first visit dislodged an unending stream of complaints about her treatment, the nursing service, her pain, ministers, religion, her doctor—everyone and everything that came to her mind. But, somehow, I had the feeling that she was afraid to stop talking—afraid if she did, she might go crazy. Her voice was angry and violent, but her eyes read panic. As I stood up from the chair, I told her that *we*, Dr. Ross and I, would be coming back to see her the next day. And we did. She became one of the many very special people with terminal illness in University of Chicago Hospital to be befriended by us. In four weeks she was actually smiling at us and other people, some of whom were complete strangers. She had begun to grow, at age sixty-eight. With terminal cancer, she was becoming a new person.

During that month, Miss Martin unfolded the power and pain of her sixty-eight frustrating years. She had struggled to become a success in business and she had succeeded, but she belonged to no one. She had no friends. Her only surviving family were a brother and sister, who lived in cities not too distant from Chicago, but who would not visit her. And no wonder. She had built up very little credit in the bank of affection with them or anyone else, for that matter. She lived a long life of isolation, possessed by her work, but giving herself to no one. We, the staff, became her family, her friends. And she began to change. She began to smile. She began to appreciate more and complain less. She actually became a joy to visit. In those few months with us she built a new life. She wrestled with her new identity as an old woman, dying alone, without anyone to care. She struggled through her grief's anger at losing all that she had in her barren world, which was now becoming enriched by others. Her angry attacks on the staff were less bitter and destructive in tone. We watched as the sixty-eight year old caterpillar became a graceful butterfly. She accepted the fact that she could not erase decades of living and magically bring about a warm relationship with her brother and sister, where no basis had been laid in their history and little potential existed in their unrelenting, rigid personalities. She could not have them, but she could have us. As she accepted her illness, she became more able to accept the human contact that was still available to her.

Thus, she could say in a seminar a month before her death, "I have lived more in the past three months than I have during my whole life. I wish I knew forty years ago what I know now. . . . I have friends. Thank you." She was *at one* with the people in her present existence, possibly for the first time in many decades, if, indeed, ever.

Miss Martin died a larger person, a person whose life was enlarged as she risked moving through the five stages of her grief process with us. And she died as she grew. Her horizons expanded to include Dr. Ross, myself, several nurses and many students from any number of disciplines who were related to the Death and Dying seminar. It was the irony of her last days that her life became richer as it approached termination. It was so and is so with many of our patients and parishioners as we help them find their way through life's last stage. I call this process, this drive toward "self-expansion", growth, our most basic human response to life.

The most important area of expansion for Miss Martin was her being allowed and willing to participate in something beyond herself—the lives of other people. This is the one level of human growth where we are totally dependent on one another. "On the physical level, we have only to maintain what we already clearly are." On this level "we do not start even with potentialities. We start with nothing. To be is to mean something to someone else. *This existence we cannot directly create for ourselves: it can only be given to us by another.*" It is a blessing.

In a group therapy session I was recently co-leading, a young woman, who knew that I was a minister asked me for a blessing. I took the request seriously since it came after my asking her if there was anything further she wanted from me. I was stunned to silence for a few minutes. I am not accustomed to being asked for blessings even in church. Then the human meaning of blessing came to me out of its historical religious meaning. The feeling of "blessedness" comes out of the experience of *being accepted.* The Christian concept of God's grace is an experienced acceptance that was unearned and unearnable. Paul Tillich describes the experience of being blessed in this way:

It happens or it does not happen. And certainly it does *not* happen if we try to force it upon ourselves, just as it shall not happen so long as we think, in our self-complacency, that we have no need of it. Grace strikes us when we are in great pain and restlessness. It strikes us when we walk through the dark valley of a meaningless and empty life. It strikes us when we feel that our separation is deeper than usual, because we have violated another life, a life which we loved, or from which we were estranged. It strikes us when our disgust for our own being, our indifference, our weakness, our hostility, our lack of direction and composure have become intolerable to us. It strikes us when, year after year, the longed-for perfection of life does not appear, when the old compulsions reign within us as they have for decades, when despair destroys all joy and courage. Sometimes at that moment a wave of light breaks into our darkness, and it is though a voice were saying: 'You are accepted. *You are accepted,* accepted by that which is greater than you, and the name of which you do not know. Do not ask for the name now; perhaps later you will do much. Do not seek for anything. *Simply accept the fact that you are accepted!* ' If that happens to us, we experience grace. After such an experience we may not be better than before, and we may not believe more than before. But everything is transformed. In that moment, grace conquers sin, and reconciliation bridges the gulf of estrangement. And nothing is demanded of this experience, no religious or moral or intellectual presupposition, nothing but *acceptance.*

Going through the five stages of the terminal person's grief is a process moving toward a blessing, "acceptance." But we are able to journey fully through the process only when we feel the "acceptance" of another person. Our "acceptance" of our own being, that is, our sensing that we are significant as a person, depends on *knowing* that we are accepted by someone or something larger than our individual self. It is at this juncture that those who minister to the needs of the dying may become physicians to the soul. It is the dying who can teach others the importance of "grace" in our lives. Acceptance is the beginning of growth.

## RELIGION AND GROWTH

Miss Martin's transformation was religious. Now, you and I may differ over what we understand religious to be, so let me first tell you how I approach religion. Religion deals with belief and ritual systems, and so do the family, industry, government, banks, the military, and all institutional interests in society. Each institutionalized interest serves a basic social and personal need. The religious issue deals with our personal need for commitment to something in which we can center our lives, something which enables us to recognize and act upon what we know is good, something which allows us to expand to our full potential as persons.

We human beings are capable of a wide range of experiences and behaviors. We can be savage and cruel on one occasion and loving and saintly on another. We can experience extreme horror at one time and be moved to ecstasy at another. We can, as Miss Martin, be rejecting and defensive at one life juncture, only to be transformed into an open, lovable person at a later time. Our capacity for "radical transformation" is one of our four most characteristic features. But the religious issue is: What in our life can keep us from the distinctive transformations and enable us to experience the greatest good our life can achieve? Religion has to do with our commitment to whatever enables us to do that. Miss Martin's "commitment" enabled her to experience her most creative potential during the last months of her life. I will come back to Miss Martin's commitment shortly. So the issue for religion is: what commitment helps us live creative lives and lessen our destructive potential?

Another characteristic we have which is basic to religious commitment is our capacity for "original experience" or personal awareness. Much of our lives, too much, is lived as "conventional experience." We force ourselves into the molds fashioned for us by our families, our employers, our friends and our public images until we experience ourselves as no self at all, but as the empty caricature of someone else's image. We lose touch with what and with who we really are. We lose touch with the freshness and vitality coming from that "original" awareness of ourselves, our own needs, our own choices. Losing this capacity we live lives of self-destruction, sometimes resulting in the destruction of those other lives we touch. Our inner conflicts, our chronic guilts, our boredoms and lassitudes, and our acute loneliness begin with our denial of our own awareness, our own "original," creative experiencing. Is there a religious commitment which will enable us to transform our borrowed identities into authentic selves? What can we commit our lives to that will help us become more authentic as persons? That is the religious issue for all, whether or not we are terminal.

Each religious faith attempts to supply a formula for the commitment which will enable us to creatively grow and transform our lives, but I have found that the actual content of a person's faith is irrelevant to whether or not they move creatively. *How* we interact with one another and *how* we experience ourselves are more important for dying persons than the content of their religious myths or their articulated philosophy of life.

Miss Martin was an agnostic. She neither believed nor disbelieved in a divine agency. The question of God was irrelevant to her way of looking at the world. As her world became more loving, as she became less destructive and more open to her own experience and the experience of others, the concept of God still remained irrelevant. There was no last minute dramatic pietistic conversion.

Dying patients are at a stage of a new transformation in their lives. They may, like Miss Martin, experience their only options as fighting in panic, backs against the wall, or giving up in despair. But even at the moment of being diagnosed as having a terminal illness, we are still human, with those possibilities for radical growth in terms of our experiencing life. But there is a cost to participation in our own radical change for the better. The price is that we become committed persons. Not committed in the sense that we become committed to a religious dogma or ritual. The commitment is an act or series of actions and is our opening up to the experiencing of who we really are in this new situation in life, not what our conventional coding of that experience tells us we feel. Miss Martin made such a commitment. After finding out that she was terminal, she still pretended to be that same rich old lady who could shout and rage to achieve satisfaction. Prior to her illness she had lived a life out of touch with her actual situation. She had built a stereotype for herself back in the early days of her business career when she did have to struggle to succeed. But when her situation changed, she continued to live according to the same old script. She had to become successful in business, but like so many of us, she became trapped in a role and gave up her capacity for original experience.

Her becoming more in touch with what was happening to her in the hospital was not something that just happened out of the blue. She had to increasingly commit herself to experiencing herself as she was, in the present, as she was in her new situation as a person approaching death. Although she had at her disposal the opportunity to work through the barriers to do her own experiencing, she did not have to do so, but took the risk and experimented with engaging with her present feelings, meanings, dreams, fantasies and perceptions. She became *committed* to the cherishing of herself as a person, valuing herself as a body knowing joy, sorrow, love, hate, confusion, clarity, being alone and being with. This commitment to experiencing our identity is basic to every transformation of our lives. If we are neurotic, living life-styles of self-destruction, our first order of business in therapy is to get in touch with our actual present experience of ourself in our present situation. Transformation of our lives for the good begins as we commit ourselves to the experiencing of our own identity, a commitment to answering the question: Who am I? Now. Here. This is the first level of religious commitment.

Miss Martin, in order to realize her full potential in this period of new transformation, had to make another commitment. She had not only to commit herself to awareness of her own original experiencing, but she had to communicate, to share that experience with others and in turn appreciate and understand the original experiences of others in her life. She increasingly committed herself to dialogue, to conversation of mutual exchange with others. She was heard and allowed herself to be heard, to be understood and understand.

We seldom think of conversation as commitment, but it is. I find that expressing what I really feel and telling another person what is actually important to me at the moment is difficult. It requires a "commitment" on my part to do so, and I sense that this is true for most of us. It is equally difficult to listen. We are usually so full of our own thoughts and responses that we seldom really listen close enough to one another to grasp the real flavor of what the other person is attempting to convey. Creative communication in depth is what allows us to experience a sense of belonging to others. It is the force that limits the destructive potential in our lives and what promotes the growth aspects. Life is a struggle. Coping with a life-time of change is a struggle, but through a life-time of change we will experience ourselves as full persons only to the degree that we allow ourselves that commitment to others which keeps us in creative dialogue. It is the way we mature. One measure of maturity is the degree to which we extend our interests and concerns beyond our immediate desire for personal comfort, and I am not suggesting that maturity is wearing a hair shirt. Human maturity, personal maturity and religious maturity, to me, all mean the same thing—can be measured by the degree to which we are able to commit ourselves to this form of human interchange. At every stage of our life, but most especially during the terminal stage, this question is the most crucial: Can I be open to expressing my original self and experiencing others doing the same thing?

This is my answer to the second problem of religion (after the problem of identity), that is, the religious problem of: What should I be committed to? What is my purpose in life? What will enable me to maximize the good? What will keep me from boredom, loneliness, inner conflict, and chronic guilt feelings? Most of our religious belief systems give us a prescription telling us to trust in God or to love one another. Creative dialogue is my way of saying similar things. Many people can express their lives in this form of dialogue and experience its benefits without calling it anything, or having a traditional designation for it. Miss Martin didn't call it anything. But after two months of practice she knew from her experience what loving and receiving love was. To be transformed, dying patients must be committed to (1) achieving a sense of their own identity through experiencing their own ongoing awareness or "original experience" and (2) committing themselves to a mutual dialogue about that experience with significant other people.

There is a third level of religious commitment which is essential to us in times of personal transformation, like that of the dying patient. At this level our prime consideration is the operational blueprint or life script we refer to in order to determine our next steps in life and to make sense of the last few. Each of us has our own special way of looking at the world and putting that experience together in some sort of coherent fashion, which helps us make sense out of what we did, are doing and plan to do. Some call this our philosophy of life, others call it our theology. Call it what you will. The name is not important. What it is is the characteristic way we go about getting what we want and how we explain that to ourselves and others. Religious commitment, the commitment to transform our lives in creative ways, regardless of our situation, requires us to have some coherent sense of the world we act in, why we do some of the things we do, and why other people act in the ways that they do. This understanding need not be articulated in any systematic way or even be entirely conscious, but it must express itself as a dominant integrating pattern in our life. Our understanding, conscious or not, must make sense of our behavior and the behavior of others. Without some sort of blueprint which makes our activities and the acts of others somewhat predictable, without a sense that we are moving in a direction that will give us more of what we want and need, and without a sense that our life has a plan or a direction, we experience our lives as fragmented and aimless.

Is it so strange to think of a dying patient as having a direction, as having a life plan? Moving and living our days with a sense of coherence is the dividend that the terminally ill patient receives for moving through the five stages. The stage of acceptance, the final stage in the transcendence of the patient, is the time when the person's life becomes re-centered and more self-reliant and self-sufficient. This is quite often a very difficult reality to face for close friends and family of the patient. An accepting person is a person who lives life with a more or less unified sense of themselves. People living committed directional lives give others the impression that they have a sense of surefootedness about their lives, a stable center, a core.

This comes from the third level of religious commitment, and answers the religious problem: In what way will I live my life? The answer may not be recited in any current poetry of a standard religious faith, and it doesn't matter if it is. What is important is whether we actually behave and experience our lives in the centered manner. When Miss Martin said, "I have lived more in the past three months than I have during my whole life," she was speaking from a centered sense of herself. She spoke from a center which gave her waning life a perspective and understanding she had not experienced before. She had grown. She had transcended one life-style for another which was more authentic to her actual situation. Her life, my life, your life—in common have a wide range of possibilities of experience and behavior. That is one of the joys and problems of being human, our seemingly endless capacity for creative change, transcendence. We are created for transcendence as birds are for flight and fish for swimming.

Living to the fullest, to capacity, to transcendence, demands that we live lives of awareness, mutual self-communication and direction. Said in another way, religious commitment has to do with the issues of: self-identity, commitment of ourselves to others and receiving their commitment to us, and a coherent, directional style of living. Our answers to three questions sum up our religious commitment. Who am I? To what do I commit myself? How do I go about living my commitment?

The answers I have given to these three questions come out of my own life experience, my reflection and reading the reported experiences of others. Verification comes from my observations of how people undergoing the most important transcendent experience of their lives, living with the imminent reality of death, respond to themselves, their situations and to others in those situations. There are patterns and the patterns bear out the above assertions.

Working with patients going through their grief process for several years, I have noticed that not everyone completes the process. Some people got stuck at one stage (see the chart of the Five Stages) and seemed to remain there until death. Some people were stuck at one place and then began to move toward resolution after a period of time. Other people seemed to move through the five stages relatively smoothly with very little intervention or support on the part of the staff.

I designed and executed a research project, hoping to gain an understanding of the religious dynamics behind the denial process and the terminally ill patient's resistance to moving through to acceptance. The most important finding for me from the study was that there was empirical support for all that we have been discussing up to now. It demonstrated that people who deny less and are more able to move through the five stages after they discover that they have a terminal illness are those people who (1) are willing to converse in depth with significant others about what their present experience is like, (2) meet others on equal terms, that is, are able to enter into real dialogue with others where both can share what is "real" with the other, and (3) accept the good with the bad. They have a framework within which the tragic and happy events of their present and past life take on meaning and give their life a sense of direction and fulfillment.

The study showed, among other things, that the process of dying is a process of re-commitment to life, coming out of a new situation. The three indicators of this re-commitment process are very much like the three attributes of the mature personality described in the writings of Gordon Allport.

The dying patient's willingness to converse in depth about his or her present awareness of memories, dreams and hopes while remaining fully cognizant of the present realities of the illness is what Allport calls "self-objectification". Allport describes self-objectivity as "the ability to objectify oneself, to be reflective and insightful about one's own life. The individual with insight sees himself as others see him, at certain moments glimpses himself in a kind of cosmic perspective." This "includes the ability to relate feeling tone of the

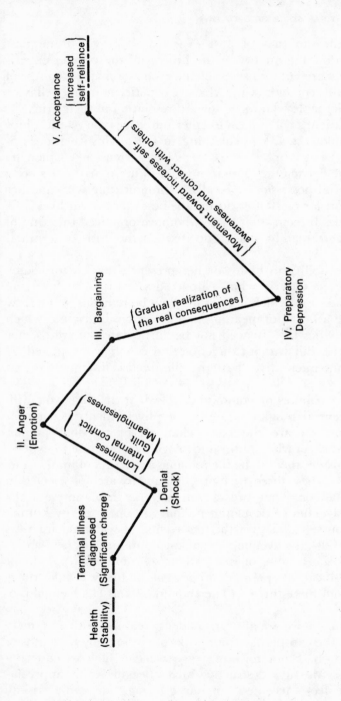

present experience to that of past experience" provided the past doesn't overshadow the quality of the process of the present experience. Allport sees present awareness of one's self as a major attribute of maturity. And this coincides with what we experience in the behavior of terminally ill people who move toward resolution of their grief.

The dying patient's willingness to enter into peer type relationships with other people instead of remaining in self-pitying relationships compares with what Allport refers to as "ego-extension", which he describes as "the capacity to take an interest in more than one's body and one's material possessions." Really communicating with another person is an effort for most of us during the best times of our lives. It is always a struggle. It seems that those who have practiced this kind of openness are more readily able to do it when the crisis of terminal illness arrives.

The patient's ability to fit his or her present situation into some meaningful life pattern is what Allport describes as a "unifying philosophy of life . . . which may or may not be religious, but in any event, has to be a frame of meaning and of responsibility into which life's major activities fit." It need not be "articulated in words, nor entirely complete. But without direction and coherence, supplied by some dominant, integrative pattern, life seems fragmented and aimless."

These three attributes or commitments, call them what you will, comprise the central religious issues of our lives. Identity, commitment, and direction are the basic channels of personal human meaning, regardless of what cultural ideologies we may use to explain them. And I consider them to be the religious sub-strata of human life. Allport says that "these three attributes of maturity are not selected in an arbitrary manner. They are chosen because they represent the three primary avenues of development that are open to any human being in the course of his growth; the avenue of widening interests (the expanding self), the avenue of detachment and insight (self-objectification), and the avenue of integration (self-unification). I doubt that any scientifically supported criteria of maturity would differ substantially from these three." (The Individual and His Religion, p. 60 ff).

Like Miss Martin, we are all transcendent creatures with extremely wide potential. We can plunge from peaks of glorious joy to depths of despairing anguish. From towering rage we can flow to caressing gentleness. Miss Martin's destructive anger became calm appreciation. When we feel "accepted" in our grieving, our denial riskily moves toward acceptance and resolution. We humans are, above all, capable of experiencing great transcendence. In dealing with significant change situations in our lives, we go through a process very much like that of the dying patient, as illustrated in the diagram of the five stages.

Learning how to live life as a dying person is not unlike the re-learning necessary after a divorce or a separation from an important person. Leaving a job or receiving an important award or recognition may begin us along the same path of transcendence walked by all of us if we have the opportunity to experience our last days of life. Religious conversion, opening ourselves to radical new life directions, will also take us along the road of the five steps. Isaiah, chapter 6, of the Old Testament is a reporting of the prophet's experiencing of those same five steps, beginning with shocked denial, moving through the emotions of awe and guilt, the redemptive bargaining, the working depression as he faces the reality of the true cost of his new commitment, to the final acceptance of his prophetic task. Paul, the Apostle, has his Road to Damascus experience and the conversion experience of Jesus is described in the Gospel of Luke, beginning with his baptism and continuing through his temptation on the mountain (Luke 3:21ff).

The "five stages" are the way of optimum growth and creative living. The three modes of human commitment and human development are our guides along the journey. We *can* live life fully until we die.

## BIBLIOGRAPHY

GORDON ALLPORT. *Personality and Social Encounter*. Boston: Beacon Press, 1964.

GORDON ALLPORT. *The Individual and His Religion*. New York: The Macmillian Co., 1950.

ANDRAS ANGYAL. *Neurosis and Treatment: A Holistic Theory*. New York: Viking Press, 1973.

THOMAS BELL. *In the Midst of Life*. New York: Atheneum, 1961.

JOSEPH HAROUTUNIAN, "Life and Death Among Fellowmen," *The Modern Vision of Death*. Ed. Nathan A. Scott, Jr.

ELISABETH KÜBLER-ROSS. *On Death and Dying*. New York: Macmillan Co., 1969.

JOEL LATNER. *The Gestalt Therapy Book*. New York: Julian Press, 1973.

HOWARD THURMAN. *Disciplines of the Spirit*. New York: Harper & Row, 1963.

# Ω

# Omega

There is no need to be afraid of death. It is not the end of the physical body that should worry us. Rather, our concern must be to *live* while we're alive—to release our inner selves from the spiritual death that comes with living behind a façade designed to conform to external definitions of who and what we are. Every individual human being born on this earth has the capacity to become a unique and special person unlike any who has ever existed before or will ever exist again. But to the extent that we become captives of culturally defined role expectations and behaviors—stereotypes, not ourselves,—we block our capacity for self-actualization. We interfere with our becoming all that we can be.

Death is the key to the door of life. It is through accepting the finiteness of our individual existences that we are enabled to find the strength and courage to reject those extrinsic roles and expectations and to devote each day of our lives—however long they may be—to growing as fully as we are able. We must learn to draw on our inner resources, to define ourselves in terms of the feedback we receive from our own internal valuing system rather than trying to fit ourselves into some illfitting stereotyped role.

It is the denial of death that is partially responsible for people living empty, purposeless lives; for when you live as if you'll live forever, it becomes too easy to postpone the things you know that you must do. You live your life in preparation for tomorrow or in remembrance of yesterday, and meanwhile, each today is lost. In contrast, when you fully understand that each day you awaken could be the last you have, you take the time *that day* to grow, to become more of who you really are, to reach out to other human beings.

There is an urgency that each of you, no matter how many days or weeks or months or years you have to live, commit yourself to growth.

We are living in a time of uncertainty, anxiety, fear, and despair. It is essential that you become aware of the light, power, and strength within each of you, and that you learn to use those inner resources in service of your own and others' growth. The world is in desperate need of human beings whose own level of growth is sufficient to enable them learn to live and work with others cooperatively and lovingly, to care for others—not for what those others can do for you or for what they think of you, but rather in terms of what you can do for them. If you send forth love to others, you will receive in return the reflection of that love; because of your loving behavior, you will grow, and you will shine a light that will brighten the darkness of the time we live in—whether it is in a sickroom of a dying patient, on the corner of a ghetto street in Harlem, or in your own home.

Humankind will survive only through the commitment and involvement of individuals in their own and others' growth and development as human beings. This means development of loving and caring relationships in which all members are as committed to the growth and happiness of the others as they are to their own. Through commitment to personal growth individual human beings will also make their contribution to the growth and development—the evolution—of the whole species to become all that humankind can and is meant to be. Death is the key to that evolution. For only when we understand the real meaning of death to human existence will we have the courage to become what we are destined to be.

When human beings understand their place in the universe, they will become able to grow to assume that place. But the answer is not in words on this page. The answer is within you. You can become a channel and a source of great inner strength. But you must give up everything in order to gain everything. What must you give up? All that is not truly you; all that you have chosen without choosing and value without evaluating, accepting because of someone else's extrinsic judgment, rather than your own; all your self-doubt that keeps you from trusting and loving yourself or other human beings. What will you gain? Only your own, true self; a self who is at peace, who is able to truly love and be loved, and who understands who and what (s)he is meant for. But you can be yourself only if you are no one else. You must give up "their" approval, whoever *they* are, and look to yourself for evaluation of success and failure, in terms of your *own* level of aspiration that is consistent with *your* values. Nothing is simpler and nothing is more difficult.

Where can you find the strength and courage to reject those outer definitions of yourself and choose, instead, your own?

It is all within you if you look and are not afraid. Death can show us the way, for when we know and understand completely that our time on this earth is limited, and that we have no way of knowing when it will be over, then we must live each day as if it were the only one we had. We must take the time, *now*, to begin—one step at a time, at a pace that makes us not afraid, but rather eager, to take the next step, to grow into ourselves. If you practice life with compassion, love, courage, patience, hope, and faith, you will be rewarded by an ever increasing consciousness of the help that can come forth if only you look within yourself for strength and guidance. When human beings "find a place of stillness and quiet at the highest level of which they are capable, then the heavenly influences can pour into them, recreate them, and use them for the salvation of humankind." *

Death is the final stage of growth in this life. There is no total death. Only the body dies. The self or spirit, or whatever you may wish to label it, is eternal. You may interpret this in any way that makes you comfortable.

If you wish, you may view the eternal essence of your existence in terms of the impact your every mood and action has on those you touch, and then in turn, on those they touch, and on and on—even long after your life span is completed. You will never know, for example, the rippling effects of the smile and words of encouragement you give to other human beings with whom you come in contact.

You may be more comfortable and comforted by a faith that there is a source of goodness, light, and strength greater than any of us individually, yet still within us all, and that each essential self has an existence that transcends the finiteness of the physical and contributes to that greater power.

Death, in this context, may be viewed as the curtain between the existence that we are conscious of and one that is hidden from us until we raise that curtain. Whether we open it symbolically in order to understand the finiteness of the existence we know, thus learning to live each day the best we can, or whether we open it in actuality when we end that physical existence is not the issue. What is important is to realize that whether we understand fully why we are here or what will happen when we die, it is our purpose as human beings to grow—to look within ourselves to find and build upon that source of peace and

---

* *The Quiet Mind*, Hampshire, England: The White Eagle Publishing Trust, 1972.

understanding and strength which is our inner selves, and to reach out to others with love, acceptance, patient guidance, and hope for what we all may become together.

*In order to be at peace, it is necessary to feel a sense of history—that you are both part of what has come before and part of what is yet to come. Being thus surrounded, you are not alone; and the sense of urgency that pervades the present is put in perspective: Do not frivolously use the time that is yours to spend. Cherish it, that each day may bring new growth, insight, and awareness. Use this growth not selfishly, but rather in service of what may be, in the future tide of time. Never allow a day to pass that did not add to what was understood before. Let each day be a stone in the path of growth. Do not rest until what was intended has been done. But remember–go as slowly as is necessary in order to sustain a steady pace; do not expend energy in waste. Finally, do not allow the illusory urgencies of the immediate to distract you from your vision of the eternal . . .*

Elisabeth K. Ross

Laurie Braga

Joseph Braga

# Resources

ALDRICH, C. KNIGHT. "The Dying Patient's Grief," *Journal of the American Medical Association*, Vol. 184, No. 5 (May 4, 1963), pp. 329–331.

ALLPORT, GORDON. *The Individual and His Religion*. New York, The Macmillan Company, 1950.

ALSOP, STEWART. *Stay of Execution: A Sort of Memoir*. Philadelphia, J. B. Lippincott Company, 1973.

ANTHONY, SYLVIA. *The Child's Discovery of Death*. New York, Harcourt, Brace & Co., 1940.

ARIES, PHILIPPE. *Western Attitudes toward Death: From the Middle Ages to the Present*. Baltimore, The Johns Hopkins University Press, 1974.

"Aspects of Death and Dying," Report, *Journal of the American Medical Women's Association*, Vol. 19, No. 4 (June, 1964).

AYD, FRANK J., JR. "The Hopeless Case," *Journal of the American Medical Association*, Vol. 181, No. 13 (September 29, 1962), pp. 1099–1102.

BAYLESS, RAYMOND. *The Other Side of Death*. New Hyde Park, N.Y., University Books, Inc., 1971.

BAYLEY, JOE. *The View from the Hearse*. Elgin, Ill., David D. Cooke, Publishers.

BECKER, ERNEST. *The Denial of Death*. New York, The Free Press, 1973.

BOWERS, MARGARETTA K. *Counseling the Dying*. New York, Thomas Nelson & Sons, 1964.

BRIM, ORVILLE G., JR.; FREEMAN, HOWARD E.; LEVINE, SOL; and SCOTCH, NORMAN A., eds. *The Dying Patient*. New York, Russell Sage Foundation, 1970.

CAINE, LYNN. *Widow*. New York, William Morrow & Co., Inc., 1974.

CAPPON, DANIEL. "Attitudes Of and Towards the Dying," *Canadian Medical Association Journal*, Vol. 87 (1962), pp. 693–700.

CASBERG, MELVIN A., M.D. "Toward Human Values in Medical Practice," *Medical Opinion and Review*, Vol. III, No. 5 (May, 1967), pp. 22–25.

CHADWICK, MARY. "Notes Upon Fear of Death," *International Journal of Psychoanalysis*, Vol. 10 (1929), pp. 321–334.

CHERNUS, JACK, M.D. "Let Them Die with Dignity," *Riss*, Vol. 7, No. 6 (June, 1964), pp. 73–86.

CHORON, JACQUES. *Death and Western Thought*. New York, Collier Books, 1963.

———. *Modern Man and Mortality*. New York, The Macmillan Company, 1964.

CURTIN, SHARON R. *Nobody Ever Died of Old Age*. Boston, Little, Brown & Company, 1973.

CUTLER, DONALD R., Ph.D. "Death and Responsibility: A Minister's View," *Psychiatric Opinion*, Vol. III, No. 4 (August, 1966), pp. 8–12.

DE BEAUVOIR, SIMON. *A Very Easy Death*. New York, Warner Paperback Library, 1973.

DE VRIES, PETER. *The Blood of the Lamb*. Boston, Little, Brown & Company, 1961.

DOBZHANSKY, THEODOSIUS. "An Essay on Religion, Death, and Evolutionary Adaptation," *Zygon—Journal of Religion and Science*, Vol. I, No. 4 (December, 1966), pp. 317–331.

EATON, JOSEPH W., Ph.D. "The Art of Aging and Dying," *The Gerontologist*, Vol. IV, No. 2 (1964), pp. 94–100.

EISSLER, K. R. *The Psychiatrist and the Dying Patient*. New York, International Universities Press, 1955.

EVANS, AUDREY E., M.D. "If a Child Must Die . . ." *New England Journal of Medicine*, Vol. 278 (January, 1968), pp. 138–142.

EVANS, JOCELYN. *Living with a Man Who Is Dying*. New York, Taplinger Publishing Co., Inc., 1971.

FARBEROW, NORMAN L., ed. *Taboo Topics*. New York, Atherton Press, 1963.

FEIFEL, HERMAN, ed. *The Meaning of Death*. New York, McGraw-Hill Book Co., 1959, pp. 114–130.

————. "Is Death's Sting Sharper for the Doctor?" *Medical World News* (October 6, 1967), p. 77.

FOSTER, ZELDA P. L. "How Social Work Can Influence Hospital Management of Fatal Illness," *Social Work* (Journal of the National Association of Social Workers), Vol. 10, No. 4 (October, 1965), pp. 30–35.

FULTON, ROBERT, ed. *Death and Identity*. New York, John Wiley & Sons, Inc., 1966.

GARNER, FRADLEY. "Doctors' Need to Care More for the Dying," *American Journal of Mental Hygiene*.

GARNER, H. H., M.D. *Psychosomatic Management of the Patient with Malignancy*. Springfield, Ill., Charles C. Thomas.

GARTLEY, W., and BERNASCONI, M. "The Concept of Death in Children," *Journal of Genetic Psychology*, Vol. 110 (March, 1967), pp. 71–85.

GINSBERG, R. "Should the Elderly Cancer Patient Be Told?" *Geriatrics*, Vol. IV (1949), pp. 101–107.

GLASER, BARNEY G. "The Physician and the Dying Patient," *Medical Opinion and Review* (December, 1965), pp. 108–114.

GLASER, BARNEY G., and STRAUSS, ANSELM L. *Awareness of Dying*. Chicago, Aldine Publishing Co., 1965.

GLASSER, RONALD J. *Ward Four Hundred Two*. New York, George Braziller, Inc., 1973.

GREEN, M., and SOLNIT, A. J. "Psychologic Considerations in the Management of Deaths on Pediatric Hospital Services," Part 1, "The Doctor and the Child's Family," *Pediatrics*, Vol. XXIV (1959), pp. 106–112.

————. "The Pediatric Management of the Dying Child," Part 2, "The Child's Reaction (vica) Fear of Dying," in *Modern Perspectives in Child Development*. New York, International Universities Press, Inc., pp. 217–228.

GUNTHER, JOHN. *Death Be Not Proud*. New York, Harper & Row, Inc.

HACKETT, T. P., and WEISMAN, A. D. "Predilection to Death: Death and Dying as a

Psychiatric Problem," *Psychosomatic Medicine*, Vol. 23 (May–June, 1961), pp. 232–256.

HARRIS, AUDREY. *Why Did He Die?* Minneapolis, Minn., Lerner Publications Company, 1965.

HICKS, WILLIAM, M.D. and DANIELS, ROBERT S., M.D. "The Dying Patient, His Physician and the Psychiatric Consultant," *Psychosomatics*, Vol. IX (January–February, 1968), pp. 47–52.

HINTON, J. M. "Facing Death," *Journal of Psychosomatic Research*, Vol. 10 (1966), pp. 22–28.

———. *Dying*. Baltimore, Penguin Books, 1967.

HOFLING, CHARLES K., M.D. "Terminal Decisions," *Medical Opinion and Review*, Vol. II, No. 1 (October, 1966), pp. 40–49.

IRWIN, ROBERT, and WESTON, DONALD L., M.D. "Preschool Child's Response to Death of Infant Sibling," *American Journal of Diseases of Children*, Vol. 106, No. 6 (December, 1963), pp. 564–567.

JACKSON, EDGAR NEWMAN. *Understanding Grief: Its Roots, Dynamics and Treatment*. New York, Abingdon Press, 1957.

JONAS, HANS. *The Phenomenon of Life*. New York, Harper & Row, Inc., 1966.

JONES, ERNEST. "Dying Together," in *Essays in Applied Psychoanalysis*, Vol. I. London, Hogarth Press, 1951.

KALISH, RICHARD A., Ph.D. "Death and Responsibility: A Social-Psychological View." *Psychiatric Opinion*, Vol. 3, No. 4 (August, 1966), pp. 14–19.

KAPLEAU, PHILIP. *Wheel of Death: A Collection of Writings from Zen Buddhist and Other Sources on Dying-Death-Rebirth*. New York, Harper & Row, Inc., 1971.

KAST, ERIC, M.D. "LSD and the Dying Patient," *Chicago Medical School Quarterly*, Vol. 26 (Summer, 1966), pp. 80–87.

KASTENBAUM, ROBERT, Ph.D. "Death and Responsibility: Introduction" and "A Critical Review," *Psychiatric Opinion*, Vol. 3, No. 4 (August, 1966), pp. 5–6, 35–41.

KNUDSON, ALFRED G., JR., M.D., Ph.D., and NATTERSON, JOSEPH M., M.D. "Observations Concerning Fear of Death in Fatally Ill Children and Their Mothers," *Psychosomatic Medicine*, Vol. XXII, No. 6 (November–December, 1960), pp. 456–465.

———. "Practice of Pediatrics—Participation of Parents in the Hospital Care of Fatally Ill Children," *Pediatrics*, Vol. 26, No. 3, Part 1 (September, 1960), pp. 482–490.

KRAMER, CHARLES H., and DUNLOP, HOPE E., R.N., "The Dying Patient," *Geriatric Nursing* (September–October, 1966).

KÜBLER-ROSS, ELISABETH, M.D. "Anger before Death," *Nursing 1971*, Vol. 1, No. 2 (December, 1971), pp. 12–14.

———. "The Care of the Dying: Whose Job Is It?" *Psychiatry in Medicine*, Vol. 1, No. 2 (April, 1970), pp. 103–107.

———. "Coping Patterns of Patients Who Know Their Diagnosis," Catastrophic Illness in the Seventies: Critical Issues and Complex Decisions, pp. 14–19. Proceedings of the Fourth National Symposium of Cancer Care, Inc., National Cancer Foundation, Hotel Biltmore, New York, N.Y., October, 15–16, 1970.

————. "Coping with Death and Dying," series of five casette audiotapes discussing fear of death, verbal and nonverbal symbolic language, stages of dying, children and death, and sudden death. Flossmoor, Ill., Ross Medical Association, 1973.

————. "Crisis Management of Dying Persons and Their Families," in *Emergency Psychiatric Care: The Management of Mental Health Crises*, eds. H. L. P. Resnick and H. L. Ruben, New York, Charles Press, 1974, chapter 8, pp. 143–156.

————. "Death," *Encyclopedia Britannica* (1974), Vol. 5, pp. 526–529.

————. "Death and the Dying Patient," an audiotape. Minnesota Nursing Home Association.

————. "Death—Caring for the Dying," an audiocassette series for the parish pastor produced by Clergy.

————. "Death: How Do We Face You?" in *Modern Perspectives in the Psychiatry of Old Age*, ed. John G. Howells. New York, Brunner/Mazel, 1975.

————. "Dignity in Death," *Medical Bulletin, Naval Regional Medical Center and Naval Hospital, Portsmouth, Va.*, Vol. 6, No. 4 (Winter, 1971), pp. 76–85.

————. "Dying as a Human Psychological Event," *Concilium: Theology in the Age of Renewal*, Vol. 4, No. 10 (April, 1974).

————. "Dying from the Patient's Point of View," *Triangle*, Sandoz Journal of Medical Science, Vol. 13, No. 1 (1974).

————. "Dying—The Final Stage of Living," an audiotape. Geriatric Symposium, New York, Hoffman–LaRoche.

————. "The Dying Patient as Teacher: An Experiment and An Experience." *Chicago Theological Seminary Register*, Vol. LVII, No. 3 (December, 1966).

————. "The Dying Patient's Point of View," in *The Dying Patient*, eds. Orville G. Brim, Jr.; Howard E. Freeman; Sol Levine; and Norman A. Scotch. New York, Russell Sage Foundation, 1970, pp. 156–170.

————. "Dying with Dignity," *The Canadian Nurse*, Vol. 67, No. 10 (October, 1971), pp. 31–35.

————. "The Experience of Death," in *The Vestibule*, by Jess E. Weiss, ed. Billie Young. Port Washington, N.Y., Ashley Books, Inc., 1972, Chapter 5, pp. 49–53.

————. "Facing Up to Death," *Today's Education*, Vol. 61, No. 1 (January, 1972), pp. 30–32. Reprinted in *Readings in Human Development 1973–74*, ed. Dushkin Publishing Group, Inc. Guilford, Conn., Dushkin Publishing Group, Inc., 1972 from *Books in Print*, pp. 258–260.

————. "The Family Physician and the Dying Patient," *Canadian Family Physician* (October, 1972), pp. 79–83.

————. "The Five Stages of Dying," *Encyclopedia Science Supplement*. New York, Grolier, Inc., 1971, pp. 92–97.

————. "Hope and the Dying Patient," *Psychosocial Aspects of Terminal Care* (1972).

————. "How the Patient Faces Death," *Public Welfare*, Vol. XXIX, No. 1 (January, 1971), pp. 56–60.

————. "Interview with—Terminal Cancer Patient," *Geriatric Focus*, Vol. 9, No. 4 (April, 1970), published by Knoll Pharmaceutical Co., Orange, N.J.

————. "The Languages of the Dying Patients," *Humanitas*, Vol. X, No. 1 (February, 1974).

————. "Lessons from the Dying," *Sociológico de la Muerte*, Madrid, Spain (1974), pp. 15–24. First published in *Tribuna Medica*, Madrid, Spain (1973).

————. "Letter to a Nurse About Death," *Nursing*, Vol. 3, No. 10 (October, 1973).

————. "The Loneliness in Dying," in *Anatomy of Loneliness*, eds. R. Audy, Y. Cohen, and J. Hartog. New York, The Macmillan Company, forthcoming.

————. "Ministering to the Terminally Ill," an audiotape. Thesis Theological Cassettes.

————. "On Death and Dying," in *The Phenomenon of Death*, ed. Edith Wyschogrod. New York, Harper & Row, Inc., 1973, pp. 14–40.

————. "On Death and Dying," NBC, November, 1974. Produced for the U.S. Catholic Conference, N.Y.

————. "On Death and Dying," Therapeutic Grand Rounds, No. 36, *Journal of the American Medical Association*, Vol. 221, No. 2 (July 10, 1972), pp. 174–179.

————. "On the Use of Psychopharmacologic Agents for the Dying Patient and the Bereaved," *Journal of Thanatology*, Vol. 2 (Winter–Spring, 1972), pp. 563–566.

————. "Problems in the Meaning of Death," an audiotape for the American Association for the Advancement of Science, December, 1970.

————. "Psychotherapy for the Dying Patient," in *Current Psychiatric Therapies*, Vol. V., ed. J. H. Masserman. New York, Grune & Stratton, Inc., 1970, pp. 110–117.

————. "The Right to Die with Dignity," *Bulletin of the Menninger Foundation*, Vol. 36, No. 3 (May, 1972).

————. "The Stages of Dying," *Php Institute of Tokyo* (November 1973).

————. "A Teaching Approach to the Issues of Death and Dying," *Archives of the Foundation of Thanatology*, Vol. 2 (Fall, 1970), pp. 125–127.

————. *To Die Today*, produced by Canadian Broadcasting Co. and distributed to institutions by Film Makers Library, Inc., New York, N.Y.

————. *Until I Die*, WTTW Channel 11, Chicago, film distributed through American Nursing Association, New York, N.Y., 1969.

————. "What Is It Like to Be Dying?" *American Journal of Nursing*, 1970.

KÜBLER-ROSS, ELISABETH and ANDERSON, JAMES. "Psychotherapy with the Least Expected," *Rehabilitation Literature*, Vol. 29, No. 3 (March, 1968), pp. 73–76.

LAMM, MAURICE. *The Jewish Way in Death and Mourning*. New York, Jonathan David Publishers, 1969.

LESHAN, L. and LESHAN, E. "Psychotherapy in the Patient with a Limited Life Span," *Psychiatry*, Vol. 24 (November, 1961), p. 4.

"Let's Talk about Death," *Christopher News Notes* (May, 1974), No. 206. 12 East 48 Street, New York, N.Y. 10017.

LIEBERMAN, MORTON A., Ph.D. "Psychological Correlates of Impending Death: Some Preliminary Observations," *Journal of Gerontology*, Vol. 20, No. 2 (April, 1965), pp. 181–190.

"Life in Death." Editorial, *New England Journal of Medicine*, Vol. 256, No. 16 (April 18, 1957), pp. 760–761.

LOVE, ANN B. "Surviving Widowhood," *Ms. Magazine* (October, 1974), pp. 84–91.

MALINO, JEROME R. "Coping with Death in Western Religious Civilization," *Zygon—Journal of Religion and Science*, Vol. I, No. 4 (December, 1966), pp. 354–365.

MANNES, MARYA. *Last Rights.* New York, William Morrow & Co., Inc., 1974.

MCGANN, LEONA M. "The Cancer Patient's Needs: How Can We Meet Them?" *Journal of Rehabilitation,* Vol. XXX, No. 6 (November–December, 1964), p. 19.

MOELLENDORF, FRITZ. "Ideas of Children About Death," *Bulletin of the Menninger Clinic,* Vol. III, No. 148 (1939).

MORITZ, ALAN R., M.D. "Sudden Deaths," *New England Journal of Medicine,* Vol. 223, No. 20 (November 14, 1940), pp. 798–801.

MUGGERIDGE, MALCOLM. *Something Beautiful for God.* New York, Ballantine Books, Inc., 1973.

NAGY, MARIA H. *The Meaning of Death.* New York, McGraw-Hill Book Co., 1965.

NORTON, JANICE, M.D. "Treatment of the Dying Patient," *The Psychoanalytic Study of the Child,* Vol. XVIII (1963), pp. 541–560.

RHEINGOLD, JOSEPH. *The Mother, Anxiety, and Death: The Catastrophic Death Complex.* Boston, Little, Brown & Company, 1967.

RICHMOND, JULIUS B., and WAISMAN, HARRY A. "Psychological Aspects of Management of Children with Malignant Diseases," *American Journal of Diseases of Children,* Vol. 89, No. 1 (January, 1955), pp. 42–47.

RICHTER, CURT P., Ph.D. "On the Phenomenon of Sudden Death in Animals and Man," *Psychosomatic Medicine,* Vol. XIX, No. 103 (1957), pp. 191–198.

ROSENBLUM, J., Ph.D. *How to Explain Death to a Child.* International Order of the Golden Rule, 1963.

———. *A Child Psychologist Talks to Parents on a Difficult Subject.* International Order of the Golden Rule, 1963.

ROTHENBERG, ALBERT, M.D. "Psychological Problems in Terminal Cancer Management," *Cancer,* Vol. XIV (1961), pp. 1063–1073.

SANDFORD, B. "Some Notes on a Dying Patient," *International Journal of Psychiatry,* Vol. 38 (1957).

SAUL, LEON J., M.D. "Reactions of a Man to Natural Death," *Psychoanalytic Quarterly,* Vol. 28 (1959), pp. 383–386.

SAUNDERS, CICELY, M.D., O.B.E. *Care of the Dying.* London, Macmillan & Co., Ltd., 1959.

———. "Death and Responsibility: A Medical Director's View," *Psychiatric Opinion,* Vol. III, No. 4 (August, 1966), pp. 28–34.

———. "The Management of Terminal Illness," *Hospital Medicine,* Part I (December, 1966), pp. 225–228; Part II (January, 1967), pp. 317–320; Part III (February, 1967), pp. 433–436.

SCHERZER, CARL J. *Ministering to the Dying.* Englewood Cliffs, N.J., Prentice-Hall, Inc., 1963.

SCOTT, NATHAN A., JR., ed., *The Modern Vision of Death.* Richmond, Va., John Knox Press, 1967.

SHANDS, HARLEY C. "Psychological Mechanisms in Cancer Patients," *Cancer,* Vol. IV (1951), pp. 1159–1170.

SHEPHERD, J. BARRIE. "Ministering to the Dying Patient," *The Pulpit* (July–August, 1966), pp. 9–12.

STEPHENS, SIMON. *Death Comes Home.* New York, Morehouse-Barlow Co., Inc. 1973.

STRAUSS, ANSELM and GLASER, BARNEY. *Anguish, A Case History of a Dying Trajector.* Mill Valley, Calif., The Sociology Press.

SUDNOW, DAVID. *Passing On.* Englewood Cliffs, N.J., Prentice-Hall, Inc., 1967.

"Telling the Relatives," *Hospital Medicine,* I (April, 1967).

THIELICKE, HELMUT. *Death and Life.* Fortress Press, Philadelphia, 1970.

TICHAUER, RUTH W., M.D. "Attitudes Toward Death and Dying among the Aymara Indians of Bolivia," *Journal of the American Medical Women's Association,* Vol. 19, No. 6 (June, 1964), pp. 463–466.

"Time, Perspective, and Bereavement." *Omega,* Vol. I, No. 2 (June, 1966).

VERWOERDT, ADRIAAN, M.D. "Comments on: 'Communication with the Fatally Ill,' " *Omega,* Vol. II, No. 1 (March, 1967), pp. 10–11.

———. "Death and the Family," *Medical Opinion and Review,* Vol. I, No. 12 (September, 1966), pp. 38–43.

VERWOERDT, ADRIAAN, M.D., and WILSON, RUBY. "Communication with Fatally Ill Patients," *American Journal of Nursing,* Vol. 67, No. 11 (November, 1967), pp. 2307–2309.

WAHL, CHARLES W. "The Fear of Death," *ibid.,* Vol. XXII, No. 214 (1958), pp. 214–223.

———. ed. *Management of Death and the Dying Patient Book: Dimensions in Psychosomatic Medicine.* Boston, Little, Brown & Co., 1964, pp. 241–255.

WARBASSE, JAMES PETER. "On Life and Death and Immortality, *Zygon—Journal of Religion and Science,* Vol. I, No. 4 (December, 1966), pp. 366–372.

WARNER, W. LLOYD. *The Living and the Dead: A Study of the Symbolic Life of Americans,* Vol. V of *The Yankee City*

WESTBURG, GRANGER E. *Good Grief.* Rock Island, Ill., Augustana Book Concern, 1961.

WEISMAN, AVERY D. "Death and Responsibility: A Psychiatrist's View," *Psychiatric Opinion,* Vol. 3, No. 4 (August, 1966), pp. 22–26.

WEISS, JESS. *The Vestibule.* Port Washington, N.Y.: Ashley Books, Inc., 1972.

WERKMAN, SIDNEY L. *Only a Little Time.* Little, Brown and Company, Boston, 1972.

WILLIAMS, ROBERT H. *To Live and to Die—When, Why and How.* Springer-Verlag, New York, 1973.

WOOLF, KURT, M.D. "Fear of Death Must Be Overcome in Psychotherapy of the Aged." Report delivered at meeting of Gerontological Society. *Frontiers of Hospital Psychiatry* (1966), p. 3.

ZILBOORG, GREGORY. "Fear of Death," *Psychoanalytic Quarterly,* Vol. 12 (1943), pp. 465–475.

# Index

## A

Acceptance of death, effect of experience with dying persons on, xvii, 79, 118, 119-121, 125-126, 128-133, 140

Acceptance phase. as stage in dying, 10*fn*, 12, 39, 100, 118, 154, 159, 160, 162

Afterlife, 38, 93, 119
in Vedic religion, 54-55

Alaskan Indians, 75, 119
attitudes toward death, 33-37

Allport scale, 79

American Indians, arrow rituals, 30-31

Anger, prevention of, 85

Anger phase, as stage of dying, 10*fn*, 11, 39, 98, 99, 118

Anxiety:
aroused by interviews with the dying, xv
and terminal patients, 80

Appreciation service, Japanese, 30

Art, and death, 2

Asceticism, as path for salvation (Hindu), 64

*Atman*, (*See also* Essential self), 61, 62
definition, 58, 59

Audiotapes, use of in Living Until Death program, 80

## B

Bargaining phase, as stage of dying, 10*fn*, 11, 39, 98, 118, 162

Bed-side service, Japanese, 30

Bedside vigil, purposes and importance of, 45

Bhagavad Gita, 71
life through death in, 60-62

Bible, 39, 41

Bitterness, prevention of, 85

*Brahmā*, 59
and origin of death, 62-63

Buddhism, 1, 2, 53, 70-71
beliefs about death, 29, 30
death, birth and liberation in, 65-71

Burial (*See also* Funerals)
Jewish customs, 46-47, 49-50

## C

Care, patient's questioning of right to, 20-22

Chaplains, 76
role of in terminal illness, 81-82, 85, 136

Characteristics predicting acceptance of death, 160-163

Children:
experience with death, 11, 19-21, 119
learning about death in Hawaii, 29
sheltered from death, 5-6

China, view of death in, 29-30, 31

Clergy (*See also* Chaplains)
role of local, 83
supportive role of, xvii-xviii, 12-13, 81-82

Condolence call, purpose of, 50

Confucianism, beliefs about death, 29

Counseling, importance of timing of, 84-85

Crying, fear of, 11-12

## D

Day of Atonement, confessions on, 45

Death (*See also* Dying)
and growth, x-xiii, 2, 33, 37, 87, 96, 97, 117, 134, 145-167
and human development, x-xi, 165-166
and life meaning, x-xiii, xvii, xix, 1, 52-72, 117, 119-126, 134, 140, 145, 147-167
as a creative force, 1-2

as central to religious thought, 1-2
as companion to life, x, 65, 71
as constructive element of life, 2-3
Buddhist doctrines, 65-71
coping with:
  in society, 5
  effect of discomfort on, 79-80, 83
  expected, 13-14
  preparation for, 84
cross-cultural views of, 27-32
denial of, 46, 47
differing cultural perceptions of, 27-32
as enemy, 53
facts and problems, 1
full experience of feelings about, xii-xiii
Hindu tale of origin, 62-63
importance of recognition of, 46
meaning questioned, x, 31-32
moral dilemma of, 41-43
questions about, xi
as rebirth, 53-64, 65-70
rituals among several peoples, 28-31
sharing of feelings about, xvi-xvii
as total annihilation, 53
treated as taboo, 10
unanticipated, 13, 14
Vedic concepts of, 53-64
withdrawal from, 92
Death and Dying Seminar, xiv-xv, xvi, xvii,
  xviii, xx, 153
Deathbed confessional:
  Jewish view of, 40, 41
  significance of, 45
Denial phase, as stage of dying, 10, 10*fn,*
  39, 80, 91, 98, 118
Dependency behavior, 18, 19
  in hospital situation, 22
Depression, prevention of, 85
Depression phase, as stage in dying, 10*fn,*
  11, 39, 99, 118
Despair, communicated by the living, xvi
Destiny:
  Chinese concept of, 31
  of human beings, 165
Discomfort scale, 78
Dying (*See also* Death)
  active volition in, 34-37
  among Alaskan Indians, 33-37
  in familiar settings, importance of, 6,
    34-37, 39, 119-121
  as a growing experience, 131, 149
  as integral part of life, 5
  Jewish guidelines for, 38-43
  as last stage of growth, 147-150
  organizational context of, 7-24
  stages of, 10*fn,* 39, 118

Dying patients:
  analysis of experience with, 79
  anxieties of, 80, 135-138
  attitude of hospital toward, 9-10
  characteristics predicting acceptance of
    death, 160-163
  importance of personal autonomy, 22-
    23, 36-37, 45, 82
  needs of, 8
  "rules" for counselors, xvii-xviii

**E**

Emotional adjustment of dying patients:
  main predicting factors, 76, 79-80
  chaplain's role in, 81-82
  family's role in, 82
  nurses' role in, 83-84
  and level of discomfort, 79
  physicians' role in, 82-83, 85
  social worker's role in, 84
  sources of help, 81
  and religious orientation, 79-80
Emotional Adjustment (EA) Scale, 77
Essential self (*See also Atman*), 56-71,
  164-167
Ethical instruction, at death, 41
Eucharist, planned celebration of by dying
  Alaskans, 34-35
Eulogy, intent of, 49
Euthanasia, 42

**F**

Facilitating funeral director, development of
  concept, 88-90
Family:
  blessing of, 41
  role in emotional adjustment, 82
Fever, as criterion for hospital care, 21
Five stages of dying, 10-12, 39, 118, 159,
  160, 162
  as applied to change and growth, 163
  in relation to hospital functioning, 10-11
Funerals (*See also* Burial), 87-96
  American, 46-47
  Chinese, 29-30
  importance of planning for, 46
  Japanese, 30
  participation in, importance for coping
    with death, 63
  purposes of, 90-91
  value of, 65
Funeral directors, possible role of, 87-96

## G

God, xviii, xix, 40, 48, 49, 51, 61, 62, 64, 84, 158
Grace, Christian concept of, 154
Grief (*See also* Depression)
  and growth, 96, 100-101
  expression of, 47, 93
  funerals and, 87-96
  levels and stages of, 51, 100-101
  repression of, effect on emotional adjustment, 46-48
  shock phase, 100
Grief work, 49-50, 89-96
Growth:
  as analagous to dying, 147-148
  dying as last stage of, 147-50
  religion and, 155-163
  through coming to terms with death, x-xiii, 2, 33, 37, 87, 96, 97, 117 134, 145-167
  as way of living, xi
Guilt, 8-9, 162
  as element in grief, 47*fn*
  expression of in expensive funeral, 47
  as grief reaction, 101
  and the professional stance, 11

## H

*Hallacha,* 40, 45, 46, 51
  framework of laws for dying, 40-43
Hawaii, death customs in, 29
Health professionals:
  changing skills and behavior of, 14-15
  current roles of, 8
Hinduism, 1, 2, 70-71
  Bhagavad Gita, 60-62, 71
  death and rebirth in, 53-64
  Upanishads, 54, 56-60, 61
  Vedas, 2, 53-56, 60
Home care personnel, role in terminal care, 84
Hospitals:
  admissions process, 17-19
  attitudes toward dying patient, 9-10
  changing role of, 7-8
  errors, 9
  as depersonalizing institution, 6, 7-24
  Living until Death Program, 73, 75-86, 119
  nurses' role, 8, 9, 11, 13-14, 17-19, 25-26, 75, 83-84, 85
  patient's dependence upon staff of, 18, 19, 22

patient's view of the patient role, 15-22
physicians' role, 8, 9, 11-14, 19-20, 75, 81-83, 85
"survival" within, 19
Human relationships, importance for coping with death, 45, 79-82, 120-121, 152-159

## I

Immortality, 57-62
Interview procedures, with the dying, 15-16
Involvement in funeral of survivors, 93

## J

Japan, death rituals in, 30-31
Jewish view of death, 1
  bedside vigil, 45
  deathside confessional, 40, 41, 45
  family, blessing of, 41
  funerals, 46-47, 49
  inevitability of death and, 41-43,
  guidelines for dying, 38-43
  guidelines for mourning, 44-51

## K

*Kaddish,* 49
*Karma,* 59, 64, 66
Krishna, 61, 62, 71

## L

Literature, and death, 2
Living:
  definitions of, xi
Living until Death Program, 73, 75-86, 119
  main problems, 85
  measures and statistical analysis, 77-79
  method and procedure, 77
  requirements, 76
  suggestions for patient care, 80-86
  summary of findings, 79-80
Loneliness, associated with grief, 100
Love, 37, 140, 157, 158, 167

## M

"Make Today Count," 118, 143
Material affairs, ordering of at death, 40, 41
"Meal of recuperation," 49-50

Mechanical life support systems, 42, 43
    removal of, 43
Meditation, Buddhist, 62, 64, 68-69
Mourning:
    Jewish guidelines for, 44-51
    mother's, 97-104
Music, and death, 2

# N

Nirvana, 66, 70
Nurses, 11, 13-14, 17-19, 75
    behavior of in climate of dying, 8-9
    role in dying patients' emotional adjust-
        ment, 83-84, 85
Nursing, dying nurse's perception of role of,
    25-26

# O

Omega, 164-67
"Original experience," capacity for, 155

# P

Pain, 21, 75, 80
    anxiety about, 83
    as criterion for care, 21
    effect on coping with death, 75, 79
"Parable of the Mustard Seed," 67-68
Paradise, Buddhist concept of, 66, 70
Patient:
    shaping of by hospital procedures, 17-22
    view of own role, 15-22
Patient-oriented procedures, 15
Philosophy, and death, 2
Physicians, 19-20, 75
    behavior of as dimension of dying, 8-9
    possible limitations on role of, 12-13
    role in dying patients' emotional adjust-
        ment, 82-83, 85, 102, 135
    responsibilities for communicating prog-
        nosis to dying patients, 82-83,
        135-136
Procedure-oriented patient care, 15
Psychosomatic illness, related to unresolved
    grief and guilt, 47, 47fn, 48, 91

# R

Rage (See Anger phase)
Rebirth:
    in Buddhism, 65-70
    in Hinduism, 53-64

Regressive behavior, and illness, 18
Religious commitment, characteristics and
    levels of, 155-62
Religious orientation (RO) categories, 78-79
Research on dying patients, ethics of, 86
"Reward-punishment" system, in hospitals,
    19-20

# S

Sacrifice, 53-54
Salvation, Hindu conception of, 62
Samoa, death customs in, 28-29
Self (See also Atman)
    attainment of in Vedic religion, 56-60
    Buddhist concepts, 66
Self-actualization, 164
"Self-objectification," 160
Shock, 91, 97, 100
Social workers, role in terminal care, xvi, 84
Society, as death-denying, xxi
Soul, transmigration of, 56
Spirits, beliefs in, 29-30
Stereotypes and roles, as growth prohibi-
        tors, 11, 117, 118, 155, 156
"Stripping process" in hospitals, 27
    definition, 16
    example, 17-19
Suffering, finding meaning in, xvii, 96, 119

# T

Taoism, beliefs about death, 29
Team nursing, 19
Terminal illness:
    ethics of research, 86
    patient's own role, 84
    preparing to cope with, 84
    role of home care personnel, 84
    role of social worker, 84
Terminal patients (See also Dying patients)
    challenges faced by, 80-81
    chaplain's role, 81-82
    communicating nature and severity of
        illness to, 39-40
    hospital care, 6-24
    study of (Living until Death Program),
        75-86
    as teachers, xiv-xvi
    needs of, xvi-xvii, 19, 22, 82, 84
Tibetan Book of the Dead, 62, 65
    teachings of, 69-70
Transmigration (See also Rebirth), 39,
        43-49, 56, 83

"Transprofessional" domain, 12
Trukese, as death-affirming society, 28

**U**

Upanishads, 54, 56, 57-60, 61
  compared to Gītā, 60

**V**

Vedas, 2, 53-56, 60
  as sacred texts, 53

Vedic religion (*See* Hinduism)
Videotapes, use of in Living until Death
  Program, 80
"Visibility" of illness, as claim to care, 21,
  22
Volition, as factor in dying, 36-37

**W**

Wake service, 30
War, experiences of, 117, 119, 122